Mingos and Sharp Parts
The Collected Wit and Wisdom of
Kenneth Calvin George Eddy

By Brian K. Eddy

1

Introduction

Introduction

You might be among the billions on this planet who do not know me and my kin…so, "Howdy"! Welcome to this snapshot of the Eddy family. It's not in Hi-Def or even very realistic. What I give you is a Photoshopped version of one small child's adventures during the first six years of his life. The colors are brighter than real life, the images, slightly less so. Oh, everything here certainly happened, just maybe not quite the way we remember.

Before the stories though, I must ask you, the Reader, for a favor. You see, I am not sure if the child is my fault or not. Psychologists and anthropologists have argued for over a hundred years about which has more of an effect on our development: nature or nurture. Are we born the way we are or do we learn all our bad habits from others? (Thanks Mom and Dad). Some say we are who we are because of our genetic makeup and it doesn't matter where we live or who raises us. Others claim we can overcome our physical or mental limitations to become whatsoever we desire. Why is this important? Because I fear that my youngest son is irreparably warped and it is all my doing. So, gentle Reader, please examine this little booklet carefully and then email me with these five words: *It's All His Momma's Fault*. Thank You.

To understand the child, and this book, I need to introduce you to him. Kenneth Calvin George Eddy was born on January 17, 2007 in Bakersfield, Ca. His parents married fairly late in life but decided that bringing at least one child into this world was an admirable quest.

Kiff, as he is known, was named for three of the most influential men in his father's life. First on the scene is the baby's paternal grandfather Kenneth L. Eddy. "Papa" is a stern but loving man who transformed himself from the stoic Deputy Sheriff with 30 years on the beat into a kind, thoughtful and generous teddy bear. All it took was ten grandchildren.

Calvin was inspired, as you might fear, by a certain comical fellow. Yes, Kiff's parents hoped that the boy would be creative, funny, brave and a founding member of *G.R.O.S.S.* just like Calvin and his tiger Hobbes.

Finally comes George, the very common name of a most uncommon man. George "the Giant" McArthur is a 7' 3" tall, 270 lb sideshow performer who specializes in sword-swallowing, fire-breathing, escapes, and dozens of other amazing feats. He is also like a brother. You may have seen him in *Big Fish* or on *America's Got Talent*. There are several amazing videos of him on YouTube and Facebook …Look him up.

Last, I would like to share the story of Kiff's birth. Perhaps not what really happened but the fable I have told the family for years. It grows bigger (if not better) with each telling. For the full effect, read it in a faintly Southern accent.

There I was asleep one night, late in Heather's pregnancy. This was my third child and I knew that once he was born I wouldn't get no shuteye for a long time. I tried to nap whenever possible. Deep in dreams I walked from room to room searching for my M&M's and sody pop.

From the shadowy corners of my mind came a faint cry, "Briiii-an."

I looked but there just weren't anyone around so I continued my search.

"Briiiiii-an."

"What!?" I cried at the ever louder voice. "What do you want?"

I'm not sure when I crossed the line tween asleep and awake. What I did know was my wife was calling for help.

"Briiiiii-an! It's time! My water broke!"

Like any good husband, I sized up the situation and made a decision. "Go get a mop!" I yelled and rolled over in the bed.

"I...AM...HAVING...YOUR...BABY!" she yelled from the open bathroom, murder in her eye.

Now that I understood who was in charge here, I was ready to take my orders.

"Well, what do you want me to do?"

"You need to call the nurse at the hospital", she barked as panic set in.

"Well allll-right."

So I reached for the nightstand, knocked off the receiver, leaned over to get it, fell out the bed, and fumbled around in the dark until I had the phone.

Riiinngggg, Riiinnnnggg

"Maternity", said a briskly efficient voice.

"Hello,MyWife'sWaterBrokeAndINeedToKn owWhatToDoNext!" I screamed in one breath.

"Did you get a mop?" she asked calmly.

I tried to be a gentleman and clarify the situation.

"No! My wife is having a baby."

We discussed the problem for quite a long time, at least 20 seconds, before she said, "I guess y'all better come on down."

"Dear," I ventured quietly, "She says we should come in. Where's your bag?"

"It's not packed yet", she replied, unnaturally calm.

I looked at her with love and understanding. "What are you going to need?"

"Just the basics", she purred.

I grabbed an overnight bag and threw in a nightdress, underwear, socks, a puzzle book and three bags of Dove chocolate. With these essentials my Heather could face the world.

We waddled out to the car and strapped ourselves in. Suddenly I was Jeff Gordon!

Out of the parking lot we flew, tires squealing through the night. We barely touched the speed bumps, one-two-three! and swung wildly around the corner. There was no one on the road so I opened up our powerful four-cylinder engine and let it roar (meow!)

I busted the first red light going forty miles an hour. We were Bo and Daisy Duke flying the General Lee over treacherous gutters, sparks a-flyin' whenever we landed. (Car didn't need that muffler anyway). The bald tires let me "Tokyo Slide" through another turn and onto the freeway.

Here's where I really made some time. My foot slammed to the floor and the tach-o-meter climbed from green to yellow to red. Smoke *trickled from the engine as we wound it up to 90 miles per hour! Whew!*

We got to the hospital and I kicked my wife out the door towards the emergency room (hey, I slowed to a gentle roll). By the time I entered the lobby, my sweet peach blossom had put an orderly in a headlock demanding morphine. I strolled up to the desk with my wild hair, crazy eyes, and green plaid lounging pants. The nurse took one look at my pink Hawaiian shirt and "explained" that the psych ward was in the next building.

I said, "No, no, no. I'm here to have a baby." They drug me off one direction and Heather down another.

After passing a Rorschach test, they let me into the room with my sweetheart. She was laying on a comfortable bed, monitors and tubes attached to her in several indecent ways and we began to wait. Then we decided it was time to wait. After we finished that we waited some more.

Finally a very pleasant looking nurse came in and told us that since nothing was happening we would be put on the list. "It shouldn't be more than 4-5 hours" she said with a smile.

In a fit of indignation I rose up and summoned all my righteous anger, looked her dead in the eye and said, "Fine! Then I'm going back to sleep! I can finish dreaming about my M&M's".

To which she replied, "And sody pop?"

I will leave you, my dear Reader, to decide if this poor child ever had a chance at a normal life.

Chapter 1
Sir Urps-A-Lot

For all our technological advances, hospitals are really a team of dedicated health care professionals, people who have given their lives to the easing of pain and discomfort. This stressful environment can sometimes lead to a bit of black humor as I was soon to discover.

They wheeled Heather into a special room filled with large and expensive equipment designed to make me think the eventual bill was money well spent. A crowd of lookie-loos gathered somewhere around my darling's ankles and took in the sights. I stood near her head and whispered encouraging words into her ear. That is until she grabbed me by the throat and whispered, "SHUT UP!"

"Perhaps she can handle this by herself", I thought.

Kenneth was delivered by c-section after he didn't fit through Heather's Southern Passage. I still recall the moment we were told the dangerous surgery would be necessary. I gripped my wife's hand very tight, told her I loved her, and everything would be fine. Then I pulled out the camera and checked to see if my lighting was good.

What? I had nothing else to do so I took pictures. The blood was a bit icky, not to mention seeing her intestines piled-up on her stomach like a German weenie roast. But what I wanted, longed to capture for posterity, was the moment of birth. After all, how often does a guy get to witness the arrival of someone from another planet? But for *that* story you'll have to read chapter 20.

It wasn't long before they threw me out, saying I could come back once everyone was stable. Idiots, there hasn't been a stable Eddy in four generations. I wasn't surprised they made me leave, it happened with both my previous children. There was some disappointment when they brought Heather back without him. I really wanted to meet that little boy.

One might think a couple more hours wouldn't matter after nine months, but though experience had taught me patience, I knew Heather would be aching to hold him the moment she awoke. Sorrow in bringing forth children indeed.

Soon the friends and family began to arrive. Though I love them all and am grateful they cared enough to visit, it was a bit like the 17-year locust invasion. Every available surface was covered with aunts and uncles dispensing good (if common) advice, nieces and nephews putting sticky fingers all over the monitoring equipment, beaming grandparents sitting back with that awful "I know what you're in for" look on their smug faces, and close friends dropping by, every last one of them asking the same question as they walk through the door, "Where's the baby and can I hold him?" What about, 'How are you doing Heather" or 'Are you in much pain"? Nobody even thought to ask the most important question of all, "Brian, can I bring you a cheeseburger or something?"

After a few days (okay maybe it wasn't that long but hey, this is my story) they escorted me back to the secret high-tech inner chambers to meet my child for the first time. I quivered with anticipation and then, rounding a corner, there he was…a burrito. Honestly, he looked like a six pound chimichanga. They had wrapped him in off-white towels and placed him under four powerful heat lamps.

"What the hel…ck is this?" I yelped.

The poor nurse misunderstood the enthusiasm of my question.

"He's doing okay," she replied hastily, "He's just not keeping his temperature up."

"What is this, a Stop-n-Rob? I'll take some guacamole and 10 gallons of unleaded."

Shamed, I must admit this was not my finest hour. Still, she was kind and let me stand with the little *hors d'oeuvres* for a while. He was so small and every time he opened his mouth, out came the tiniest little squeak, like a

cute furry little mouse being stepped on by hiking boots.
Everybody knows that sound, don't they?

The grand introductions took place some five
hours after Kenneth arrived on our planet
(remember…chapter 20). Mommy was joyful, Nana cried
and Papa cuffed me on the shoulder saying, "Maybe you
aren't a complete waste of skin like I thought". It was a
scene of perfection and everyone was happy.

The End

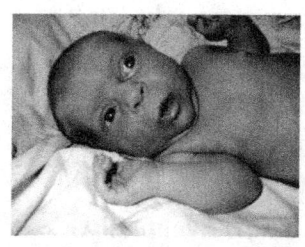 Not quite. At this point
in our story I must introduce the
anti-hero. Kenneth Calvin
George Eddy looked a bit like
Kermit the Frog without all the
endearing cuteness. In fact he
greatly resembled Lord Voldemort at the beginning of
Harry Potter and the Goblet of Fire. He was small,
wrinkled, with an over-sized hairless head, and required
feeding every few hours.

Eventually our little family moved from the
birthing rooms (which, by the way we didn't use so why
did I have to pay for them, huh huh huh) to a recovery
room. There Heather tried to relax after doing a fairly
good imitation of John Hurt in Alien (watch for the movie
references). The tiny beast latched itself onto her

repeatedly and drained what remaining strength she had for its own selfish needs. Soon after the first of these assaults I discovered the true nature of this *thing* we had brought into our lives.

Heather nursed him for a couple minutes and then announced, "He needs to burp." I'm not really sure how she knew this. Did they have some odd telepathic connection? Had I missed the baby throwing his shoulders back and doing that weird chicken-head-bop thing that precedes a massive belch? Regardless, she detached him from her bosom, tossed him over her shoulder and began thumping him energetically on the back.

But something was wrong. He wouldn't burp. No matter how hard she smacked him or how often, he just lay there making that "waa-waa-waa" sound that drills right into the base of every man's skull. Eventually Heather turned to me for help. Actually, I took the kid from her because *obviously* she was too inept to handle the situation.

One…two…three light taps and he expelled all the air which had invaded his tiny little stomach. Out too came the milk, the water and I could have sworn Jimmy Hoffa tumbled to the floor but memory's a bit hazy on that one. Well, not unusual to get vomited on occasionally. I had two other kids and they showered me with various bodily fluids many times. No big deal.

That is until it happened again. And again. And again. I can say without fear of contradiction that the little troglodyte threw up Every-Single-Time-We-Fed-Him. To this day I don't know how he survived. Science tells us it is physically impossible to gain mass over time when immediately after eating one purges a greater volume than was ingested. We had our very own anorexic and he wasn't even three days old yet.

We held a beautiful ceremony. The whole family was there and Heather looked radiant. I cradled the child in my arms, gently nuzzled the top of his head and then spoke in a clear strong voice, "For the exceptional work you have done in keeping the hospital laundry staff employed and for breaking new ground in the field of regurgitational research, I am pleased to bestow this title and rank upon you. I dub thee…Sir Urps-a-lot!" We had to work very hard at finding just the right title for him. Darth Vomitus was a strong contender though we rejected Sir Pukes-a-lot out of hand.

He certainly earned the honor because our child just never stopped. He puked from water, from breast milk, from formula. Only after six months did I realize what he wanted was Diet Pepsi because that was all he got from his mother during gestation. But we don't talk about that.

Heather and I clung to the ridiculous hope that once we had the little "darling" home his stomach might settle down. Surprisingly, his frequency and volume of hurlage only increased with time. All joking aside, I began to get worried. This couldn't be good and if it kept up I would take him back to the hospital and ask for a refund. Obviously they gave us a defective model.

As the first week passed and we grew accustomed to the smell of curdled breast milk, our fears lessened. The kid seemed happy and healthy. He was curious, active and ate like a pig. If not for the continual flow of cottage cheese coming back up, our child was perfect.

Granted, we felt a bit of shame that he NEVER had clean clothes. Neither did Heather nor myself for that matter. But we were happy and he was loved. Sir Urps-a-Lot reigned over us peasants for six more months.

Chapter 2
The Hockey Puck

Imagine if you will a hockey arena. The seats are a deep burgundy; the huge cubical scoreboard seems to float over a sheet of brilliant white ice; and 8000 screaming blood-thirsty fans alternately rage at the officials and bellow ecstatic cries of victory to their team. This of course was the peaceful, nurturing environment we wished to bring Kiff into upon the occasion of his first week in the world.

His mother and I are not what one would call fanatics. We enjoy as many games as we can and my extended family members are multi-year season ticket holders. But we don't dress-up or threaten the other team's fans. One might say it was predestined that the child would find his way to the rink eventually. I like to think he enjoyed the experience. But to be honest, he did't pay *that* much attention to the game.

We trooped in carrying our personal bags with

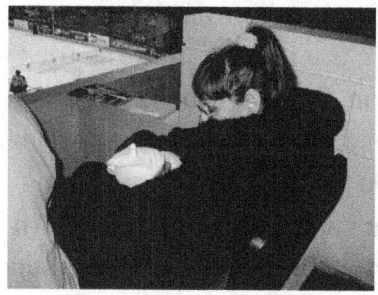

assorted books, water, candy (shh, don't tell the management) and sundry other items. We also bore the indispensable diaper bag. Anyone who has ever taken an infant anywhere will certainly recognize the absolute necessity of that piece of luggage.

Though only a week old, Kiff had already made it very clear he would brook no disruption to his routine. Accordingly, within 20 minutes of warming our seats, he spewed all over my shoulder. Luckily I was prepared. No fewer than 10 burp rags sat in the bag and passed one of them with the child as a matter of course. Still, the feeling of warm, partially digested milk trickling down my neck was (and is) one of my more unpleasant memories.

We had an enjoyable time. That is until the players skated out on the ice for their warm-ups. Music, loud throbbing soul-crushing music leapt out of the massive speakers. Kenneth, who was taking his 37th cat nap of the day, jerked awake and began craning his neck around wildly.

Now I understand that infants that young simply do not have the muscle needed to look around. They don't have the control. Heck, I doubt if they even realize there are things are outside themselves. But this kid KNEW there was music and he wanted to discover the source.

Heather pulled him close to her bosom and tried to comfort as only a mother can. But Kenneth had other ideas. She cooed and he cried. She covered his ears and he jerked his head from side to side. She wrapped him firmly in the blanket and he kicked for all his worth. All the while his head kept turning further and further around.

I thought Beetlejuice decided to come visit our little family. I hoped not because I was lousy at the Calypso.

His fascination with the noise though was nothing, *nothing* compared to how he was enthralled by those

 bewitching lights. The otherwise drab atmosphere was torn apart by searing bright message boards that flickered, rolled, spun and chased each other around the arena. Kiff was mesmerized.

Finally, because we'd tried everything else, Heather turned him to face the crowd. Instantly his whole demeanor changed. He laughed in that squeaky little voice. He danced to the music with better rhythm than I have today. And he watched. His little eyes followed the spotlights as they zipped around and around. I know it may seem impossible but that kid did it all. Even I thought it was weird. My doubt was quenched however when the flashing stopped with the puck drop and he opened up with a full on tantrum.

Hockey isn't the most popular sport in the world. And while this news may shock some areas of the Great White North, for the rest of the world, soccer is king. What many do not realize is there are fundamental similarities ('dey look alike' for you folks back home) between the two games. There is a scoring net at either end which a player defends; rules about how and when a player may pass certain lines on the field; even some of the penalties resemble each other. On a deeper level, the fans share a common experience. Capable goalies and frequent changes of possession result in low scoring games being the norm. 1-0 and 2-1 are seen far more often than 6-5. Because of the limited opportunity for celebration, tension runs very high until a goal brings out a wild, raucous party.

What does any of this have to do with Kenneth? If memory serves, his debutante game had a very high score. The home team won with five tallies while the visitors made three. This gave me eight chances to observe his reaction to the general chaos around us. Would he be scared by the yells and emotional outbursts? Would he cry or try to hide his face? Sadly, he did all those things…but only when the home town Condors scored.

Almost as if he belonged not to us but some other family making a road trip, Kiff let out a wail like something from the depths of Hades with every Condor's goal. "But he was just startled by the sudden noise and jubilation," you might say. "No, no, no," I reply. "For his sobbing lasted precisely from the moment of the score until the puck was dropped again and play resumed." In other words, he knew what was going on and had chosen to root for the other team.

If any further proof were needed, when the visitors scored and the entire arena erupted in curses, jeers and moans of disappointment, Kiff merely lay there cooing to himself wearing that smug little grin which I would soon learn to fear (chapter 21).

By on odd coincidence, that evening also happened to be a 'meet and greet' event. After the game season ticket holders were escorted into the building's inner chambers and allowed to visit with the warriors whom they had so lately cheered. We spent a pleasant hour making empty small talk with tired and distracted 22-year olds who would much rather be at the bar down the street, chatting-up a few "wanna-be's" who hoped to become WAGs.

The evening was far gone by the time we headed for our car and unexpectedly ran into some booster club members of the opposition, come down to see their boys lose. My mother and oldest son were ardent defenders of good sportsmanship and so, somewhat untruthfully, told the disappointed guests it had been a good game.

A nice conversation bloomed between my mother and the matriarch of their crowd. Soon Nana had begun telling her of Kiff's odd behavior. She was appropriately amazed by his antics and bemoaned that she could not bring her own newly arrived grand-daughter on trips.

In a fit of hijinks I leaned in close and offered to give her the little traitor as a mascot. He certainly appeared to like the Stockton Thunder far more than our own beloved Condors. Everyone laughed heartily and parted company on friendly terms.

Not for the last time did I miss the chance to free myself of a potentially deadly enemy. Little did I know that within that wiggling body lie a soul of immense evil. And so I drove home in blissful ignorance of the dangers I faced in the years ahead (remember chapter 21).

Chapter 3
Binky Boy

Sometimes, in the dead of night, I awake remembering the binkys. I still sweat in fear of them. For two years of my life they were everywhere. You might know them as Noms, Nuks or the classic Pacifiers. We bought them by the truck load and Kiff loved each and every one with a passion to rival Messalina.

 At first I saw no harm in the little bits of plastic and rubber. I know dentists and pediatricians have begun to fret about warping the child's palate with over use but they certainly stopped the little siren from going off every ten seconds. Sleep was at a premium so we risked the danger in order to get a few precious hours in the arms of Morpheus. They were a godsend as far as we were concerned.

Yet over time I began to fear he might like them too much. From the first moment he got one into his pudgy little mouth we knew this was a love affair for the ages. Perhaps Kiff's favorite game was to tuck the handle of his binky up under his nose and then wriggle his mouth wildly. This shook his whole face and made him look like a piglet snuffling around for truffles. Meal times were an adventure as it took three union thugs, two pry bars and a pneumatic jack-hammer to pull the darn thing from his mouth. Lord forbid you should set it down within reach or he would pop it back in between bites. One time it got cemented in by warm oatmeal.

***

Any parent can tell you there comes a moment, one only seen while looking back, when the sleeping/eating/pooping machine in their home suddenly becomes a person. There is a reason they call it 'personality'. To my shock, Kenneth had opinions and wants beyond what *we* had been providing. It was at this time I noticed our son was now an individual.

Because of that moment this book will now change as well. Short stories shall replace the narrative and Kiff the Person replaces Kiff the Object.

Hold on…it's gonna be a wild ride.

***

During his second year I seriously thought my son had no mouth. Instead, he possessed a plastic protuberance where a normal mouth should be. It magically changed colors, size and gained or lost a small handle. I even considered taking him to the doctor for a binky-ectomy but I wasn't sure it was covered by my insurance.

***

At first Heather and I were fighting a losing battle though we didn't know it. When I said we bought them 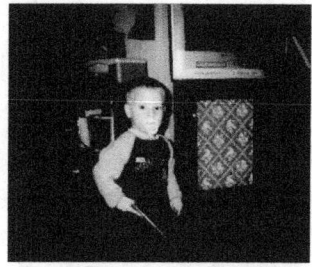 by the truckload, I wasn't exaggerating. Every time we went to the store, particularly the Dollartree/99 Cent store, we almost automatically grabbed a couple packs of binkys. Some perverse, almost selfish desire to never be without one (and a couple back-ups) meant we eventually had a Nom in every purse, pocket and bag; *plus a couple back-ups*. A half dozen rattled around my car and don't get me started on his diaper bag which had one in every pocket and two on straps hanging over the side.

Heather and I decided the time had come for a slow widening of the gap between kid and *faux nipple*. We tried waiting until late in the day to give him one; pulling it out after a couple hours of relentless sucking; and only let him have one at bedtime after all other options were exhausted. He grew livid about the whole experiment. His reaction though wasn't to scream bloody murder until his blessed friend was returned, not our Kenneth. No, he began to scheme. I would have been far more afraid then if I knew what I know now.

***

Looking back I see we handled the situation poorly. If you're gonna take something from a child, especially if you have dozens of them in the house, and you can't just say, "No more". You have to get rid of all you can and prevent the child from finding any you may have missed. But of course Heather and I didn't do that.

We planned to take the darn things from him over time but I had no idea how long that would be. For months we were faced with the same little drama: Kenneth playing in 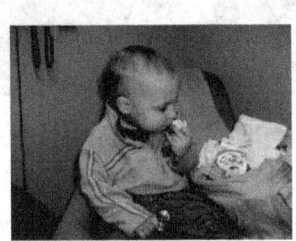 another room and it would get quiet. Any parent of a toddler knows that silence is not golden but the undeniable signal of trouble and often impending bloodshed. Heather and I would rush about the apartment looking for the kid. Almost every time we found him sitting contentedly noshing on a binky in some dark corner. We'd take the infernal thing and quietly, out of his sight, throw it away. If we didn't buy any more and slowly disposed of them, eventually they would all be gone...right?

***

Kenneth is a criminal mastermind. Once he cottoned on to what we were doing the binkies, which had infested the house, suddenly disappeared. I assumed Heather was gathering them while she believed the same about me. What neither of us guessed was that *he* had begun hiding them from *us*.

Soon binkies popped-up in the oddest places. Heather found one stuck between the towels in the linen closet. I found another resting in the back of his sock drawer. We discovered binkies behind plants, inside dishes, next to the TV and floating in the cat's water dish. I shudder to think of that one. As our victories mounted, Kenneth decided to escalate the War of the Binkies.

He sidled into the living room late one evening looking supremely happy. I'd developed a healthy distrust of anything that made him smug so I asked what he was doing.

"I have a binky."

"No you don't."

"Yes I do."

"No Kenneth. There is no binky in your mouth. There is no binky in your hand. In fact, there are no binkies in your pockets because you have no pockets because all you have on is your underwear."

He smiled broadly and reached down the back of his briefs to pull out a pacifier. It was in his mouth before I could react.

"Noooo! Give me that!"

I took the dratted thing and tossed it onto the table.

"Kenneth Calvin, you *have* to learn to get along without those things."

He kept smiling.

As I turned to look at Heather he reached into the *front* of his underwear and pulled out another binky which soon followed the first into his mouth…and then onto the table.

I took him into my arms and gave him a light swat on the rump only to have my hand start stinging. What was in there? I peeked into the shorts and saw not only two more binkies but a book and some jacks. He had armored himself against the inevitable punishment!

Gotta give him credit for thinking ahead.

***

One of the worst parts of any addiction is the withdrawals. At first there's the emptiness, an undefined need. If your drug of choice (be it alcohol, caffeine or binkies) is available then the answer is clear. But what if your chosen medication can't be had? The gnawing inside grows to a longing. Soon you feel madness forming. You would do anything, anything to get just a bit of that joy juice because then everything would be better. You would sell, steal, kill just to be rid of this pain, to be whole again.

Then when you finally get a little taste of what you've been craving it's impossible to hold back. Like a man on the edge of starvation you grab every morsel you can and take it all at once. That feeling of being alive again is overwhelming and you sink into blissful oblivion. Maybe you lay back in a swoon or perhaps you laugh and laugh and laugh.

Kenneth loved to find a stash of binkies all at once.

***

Heather is the disciplinarian of our family. I get fixed on what I'm doing, even if it is nothing at all. So I often miss the beginning of a problem. Alex and Mack start to bicker or Kiff doesn't pick-up his toys right away and I, to quote Dory, have "nuthin' in my noggin". You could say it's my incredible ability to focus. Brian's train of thought going off the rails is a bit closer to the truth. Thus the tension level in our home will already be at six or seven before I know anything is going on. Heather jumps in and handles it while I am chasing around behind trying to figure out what's happened.

So here I am, in a mindless stupor, and Kiff runs into the room. In his mouth is a very familiar looking binky. I stare at him for a moment before remembering I took that one from him not 10 minutes before. Right behind him is Heather trying to wrench it out of his jaws. The squeal of protest is piercing. I leap to my duty as father and head of the house.

"Give me that!" I order and reach for the small handle.

His head spins in every direction and quite around to avoid losing his precious nom. Words spill from his lips but only "binky" and "mine" are understandable.

Finally I extract it and, despite his cries of utter horror, I toss the thing into the kitchen trash amongst the curdled yogurt and rancid spaghetti. His anguished cry echoes around the neighborhood. Oh the humanity! The cruelty! How could his own father be such a monster? Then strangely he calms down, gives his mother one last hug for consolation and ambles off to his room.

I think, "Problem solved. He's finally learning" and I settle back onto the couch in a self-satisfied glow.

Later Kiff walks into the room. In his mouth is a very familiar looking binky. I stare at him for a moment before remembering I took that one from him 10 *and* 20 minutes before.

"Kenneth! Where did you get that binky from?"

Calm as you like he took me by the hand and led me to the kitchen where he pointed into the bin.

Ask a stupid question.

***

Kiff's resourcefulness knew no bounds. During those days of the Great Weaning he would cry incessantly for a Binky. We couldn't take him into the baby section of a store because sure enough, the moment he saw those damn things on the shelf he would snatch at them and start trying to gnaw on the package. We learned to swing the cart wide out of his reach.

One day at Wal-Mart (yes, we shop at Wal-Mart) he was having a rough time. The constant whining, begging, and pleading caught the attention of other shoppers. Not to mention how Kiff was acting.

We meandered around lost in our shopping. Then Heather realized Kiff was no longer whimpering. We glanced at each other and then at the kid. There in his effervescently happy, slightly drooling mouth was a binky! It was pink and yellow with little duckies all over it.

This was impossible. We frisked him thoroughly before leaving home and went nowhere near the infant's department.

Then down the aisle we saw a 6 month old girl in a pretty pink and yellow Easter dress winding up her scream and mom looking desperately at us. It seems as we passed each other, little sticky-fingers had plucked the baby's binky right out of her mouth!

Oh the shame.

Chapter 4
Ungeheurlische Kinder*

There is simply no way to tell stories about Kenneth without eventually running into his brother and sister. Alexander and Mackenzie are the offspring of my first marriage. As this book is about Kiff and not me, I won't bore you with the tedious details of that part of my life. Suffice it to say we had our differences, I made some major mistakes and we are no longer married. However, out of all the kerfuffle I did gain two wonderful…er great…um lovely kids.

***

 Alexander James Eddy was born in late October 1997. He is, was, and always shall be obsessed with sports, particularly baseball. I have a great home video of him (age 3) and me taking batting practice in the living room. I tossed the wiffle ball and he tried to hit it. He was actually quite good and soon made contact every time. After getting a "hit" he would run down the hallway and slam headfirst into the end wall screaming "safe"! Perhaps I should have worried a bit more. Nah…his mother's genes.

Today Alex is a strapping 15 year old who likes video games almost as much as sports. Girls are becoming a close 3rd, though I don't want to think about that. He also holds the best job any boy possibly could…the object of his little brother's hero worship.

The sheer joy in Kiff's voice as he sings praises to Alex's name is at once heartwarming and wrenching. They only get to spend a couple hours together on Thursdays plus every other weekend. I pray it is enough to build that brotherly love they both deserve.

***

Mackenzie Rene Eddy is every bit the older sister. She's a bossy know-it-all who, unfortunately for the baby, usually does know what she is talking about. Therefore her relationship with Kenneth is usually getting him to play what she wants, how she wants and when she wants. For now it works because he loves her nearly as much as he does Alex. We'll see what happens in a couple more years.

She was born in 2000 and, as an "April Fools" baby, has made a fool of me. With just a bit of cajoling and the right amount of eyelash flutter, she can often get what she wants. I'm just glad Heather is here to keep things sane.

Like many 12-year-old girls, Mack is into clothes, boys, music, boys, art, boys and of course, did I mention BOYS? At this point I would like to insert a nifty little thought I saw on Facebook not too long ago: When your daughter starts dating, shoot the first boy. Word will get around.

***

Now teenagers, the older two are very concerned about their image. They are easily embarrassed and hate when I tell "cutesy" stories about them. I know this chapter is going to be absolute torture when (hopefully) millions of perfect strangers read it. So I decided that, if I am going to make their lives a total wreck by shaming them before the whole world, I may as well do it right.

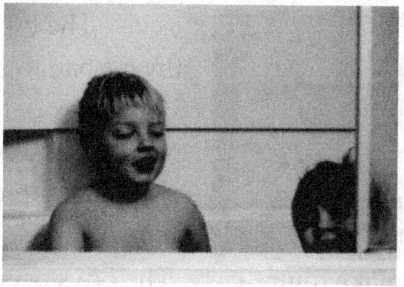

So now I present a few vignettes starring Alex, Mack and Kenneth. May we all live long enough to see them reach adulthood.

***

The only person disappointed when Kenneth came to our family was Mackenzie. She very much wanted a baby sister. Her view was: since her mother had produced a son with the new husband it was only fair Heather and I should have a girl. Even so, there has never been any resentment or anger about Kiff. Actually, they are all talking about us having another one…gah, like its open to a vote.

***

Alexander is completely thrilled about having another baby brother. That makes one with his mother and one with me. He thinks he's winning: three boys to two girls in each family.

***

 The boys have always had to share a room. Since Alex only spends every other weekend with us it's hardly a problem. I thought a nice set of bunk beds would make things easy. The boys decided to handle things their own way.

***

AJ and Mack were very good with the new baby. He stayed out of the way and she wanted to hold Kiff all the time. Neither was willing to change his diaper…ever. They both enjoyed feeding him though. How often does a pre-teen have *carte blanche* to make a mess and blame it on the little one? They also liked to help dress him. Or I should say, offer advice on what the kid should wear.

We had three clothing options: onesies with food stains; onesies with milk stains; and onesies with both. It was impossible to match the color of cloth so we settled for coordinating a nice meal.

At least people would think we were feeding him a balanced diet.

***

I thought he was a bit slow in learning to walk. For about 6 months Kenneth thought he was an infantryman. Huh, I wonder if that is where they got the name for soldiers who crawl on their bellies like babies who can't walk yet. *Infant-ry-man.*

Anyway, at first he rolled around and around in circles because he couldn't move his big fat head so well. He even got a rug burn on his noggin once from trying. When he learned to straighten out though, he was off to the races.

His brother and sister used to have endless fun playing a live 'video game' by putting various obstacles in Kiff's way and seeing how he would work around them. Each would have a goal and get to move a block in turn to direct Kiff across the room. They scored points when the baby reached their goal and ended when he sat down to bawl in frustration.

***

Things got interesting after he became mobile. I never knew *exactly* where the little rugrat was but we were confident in the door gates and screens. To find him we just had to follow the trail of destruction. Easy peasy.

An integral part of our infant gulag was the security screen installed by our apartment complex. It was fairly good quality and we enjoyed leaving our wooden door open to entice any faint zephyr which might come our way. For anyone not familiar with Bakersfield in the summer, imagine the driest, hottest, most desolate corner of Hell…that's where you would vacation if you lived in Bakersfield.

My only problem was the older two kids liked to open said screen door and go play in the portico outside. They'd draw on the concrete, bounce balls, *and take absolutely no thought to whether they had left the door open and allowed the baby to wander away!*

One beautiful summer's afternoon I decided to do some dishes (yes it's true). The kids were in the living room watching TV and Kiff was safely nestled between them. I poked my head in occasionally, just to make sure they were all there. In a fit of insane fatherly love I even took them a plate of cookies to munch on and then retreated to my scouring pads.

Not five minutes later I suddenly realized the place was quiet…too quiet. With trepidation I peeked around the corner to find the other room completely empty. As Mrs. Weasley might have shrieked, "No note! Baby gone!"

I rushed to the door which was standing wide open and saw the two erstwhile sitters playing with bubbles outside.

"Where's Kenneth?" I asked through gritted teeth.

"I dunno", they answered.

"You had him just a second ago", I replied, my calm exterior beginning to crack.

"Maybe he's inside."

"He's NOT inside. There is nowhere inside he could be except the living room and I just walked through there."

At this, my two kind and helpful children (aged ten and seven and hardly capable of being on their own) bolted off in opposite directions yelling, "Kiff! Kenneth!" In moments they had disappeared around separate corners.

Great! Now I had a preteen, a kid and a toddler all roaming aimlessly through the grounds. I took off after the girl because I knew I could catch her first. She had made a bee-line for the swimming pool and was almost to the protective fence when I caught up. After confirming that the baby was not floating inside I turned my attention to Mack.

For modesty's sake I will omit the choice words I shared with her. Suffice it to say I wanted her back in the apartment forthwith. Then off in the distance I heard Alex yelling for Kenneth. His voice echoed weirdly through the halls and it required several bellows of my own to get his attention. He was sent packing as well.

Finally I could turn my thoughts to the worst problem. I whirled on the spot looking for any sign of the escapee and there, in the one direction none of us had tried, approached a neighbor from 15 apartments away, my dear Kiff in her arms. How a baby who barely knew how to walk managed to get so far in just a few minutes I'll never know.

I ran to her, thanks pouring from my lips profusely, and took him back. I should say I tried to take him back but he wanted nothing to do with his daddy. Being with the attractive blond from across the way was perfectly fine with him, thank you very much.

Those who lived near us may have thought the screams were from a terrible thrashing I gave our three little Eddy's. Fact of the matter is I didn't lay a hand on any of them. Kiff just wanted to go back and spend time with the pretty lady.

***

Near our home lies a nice park. It has all the usual slides and swings which children love so much. What it also is a ring of very steep hills. Imagine a swimming pool about 300 yards wide and 500 yards long. I think they built it in the bottom of a natural sump pit or storm drain. I know it floods anytime we have more than a quarter inch of rain. Luckily that only happens every five years or so.

The kids just love to visit this park and either run or roll down the hill. I cannot tell how many times I have warned them to be careful but do they listen? After one particular day when Alex almost toppled over headfirst, I laid down the law.

"Alex, I don't want you running down that hill anymore. You could fall and that grass isn't as soft as you think. You could break your neck."

He just nodded and went off to the toys.

Later I saw him and the baby standing on top of the hill again.

"Get down here right now!" I hollered.

So they did. Kiff riding Alex down the hill like a sled.

***

For about two weeks in the spring and another two weeks in the fall, Bakersfield has some very pleasant weather. We took family walks whenever it was nice out and the kids loved it.

41

Our apartment lay just a few blocks from Alex and Mack's maternal Great-Grandmother's house and so we would stop in and check on her whenever possible. Margaret and I had always gotten along well enough and though the divorce was ugly, she still treated me kindly.

As we strolled through the neighborhood our kids would run ahead, playing the impromptu games that children do. Usually of the make-Kenneth-think-we-are-leaving-him-behind sort. I hated it when my brothers played that game with me.

Heather and I took one very sensible precaution during these evening walks. We endowed each child with several glow sticks so they would be clearly visible to us and oncoming drivers. Alex and Kiff naturally would sword fight while Mack created a whole line of fashion bracelets, earrings and tiaras.

One night we started pretty late and it was fully dark before reaching the half-way point in our journey. Nevertheless we trudged on with determination. There were no cars anywhere and in such a quiet block we didn't worry a whole lot when the kids ran about like total loons.

Off ahead of us were AJ and Kiff when suddenly they both fell headfirst on the street. Kenneth was crying loudly and Alex whimpered as I ran forward to check on them.

When I approached they turned to their father for comfort but I had frozen in shock. Their faces were a bloody mess. At least that's what I thought for a second until I realized that even *my* kids' blood didn't glow in the dark and shouldn't be red and blue and green and yellow!

The dirty little sneaks had bitten through the glow stick casing and smeared themselves with the chemicals and then faked their own injuries! It should have been a sign of things to come.

***

Need I say that all three kids might be slightly touched in the head? Some months ago I was reading quietly when giggling erupted from the kitchen. This never bodes well.

Through the door walked Alex and Mack, carrying their baby brother by the arms and legs, chanting like zombies, "Hu-man Sac-ri-fice. Hu-man Sac-ri-fice."

I suppose that makes me Gomez Addams.

***

My children love each other a lot and they often work together on projects. The boys usually have a specific goal be it sports, video games or something a bit more sinister (Chapter 21). Mackenzie and

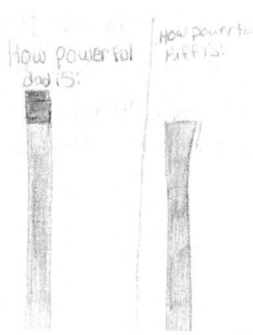

Kenneth however are more into the role playing games.

Recently she explained to him about power and strength. Kiff wanted to know how powerful he was and so Mack drew him a picture:

Please note the addition to my level after I complained about being even with a five-year-old.

***

Mack likes to play teacher to Kiff or run the "Mackenzie Store" where the kid gets to learn all about consumerism. Often she sells him stuff belonging to us parents. But since they use fake money I suppose everything evens out.

***

Sometimes I have to work on a Saturday. One of these happened shortly after we bought our house. Everything was still packed-up and Heather had to deal with the kids alone. Obviously with Dad away it was the perfect time for everyone to head for the boy's closet and draw all over the walls.

The family portrait is cool and that volcano looks lovely. But what's the deal with the helicopter-car? Those blades are nowhere near capable of providing the lift needed to fly. Sheesh

***

Round and round the mulberry bush, the Kenneth chased the Kinzie

The Kenneth thought twas all in fun
Smack went the Kenzie.

We have two Mulberry trees in our backyard. I grew up with a fruitless Mulberry and it never occurred to me that there might be a *fruited* variety. What an idiot. Imagine my surprise the first time our trees came out in

millions of little berries.

After checking the Internet to be sure they were edible I set the kids loose on them. Alex ate a couple fistfuls and then wandered back inside to play video games. Mack and Kenneth made a day of it.

Heather and I watched in amusement for about 10 minutes as they ran about snatching greedily at the low-hanging fruit. The two of them looked like Augustus Gloop and Verruca Salt entering Willie Wonka's factory.

Soon they began running circles about the trees and throwing berries at each other. By the time they were finished every bit of them was smeared with sticky juice and tiny black seeds. Their clothes were stiff with sugar and both had enormous smiles.

I didn't have the heart to warn them of the inevitable tummy aches they would have that evening.

***

To understand this next story, you have to know my two older brothers are Willie and Damon.

Sometimes Alexander can't help being a big brother. He will pester the younger kids incessantly and whine about how much they bug him. Kenneth ran in crying, "Alex gave me a Dry Damon!"
We looked at each other in utter confusion until Heather asked, "Do you mean a Wet Willie?"

"Noooooooooo. He didn't put any spit on his finger before he put it in my ear."

Yuck.

***

46

We bought a Wii. Some of you might not be into video games so I will explain. The Nintendo Wii is a game console like the PSP, X-Box or Atari 2600 for you old fogies. It has a unique feature however. The game controller is wireless *and* the game follows your hand movement. For tennis I would serve just like normal. For baseball I would swing away. The technology is amazing.

I installed the unit amid raucous screams of delight. Alex and Mack had a Wii at their mom's and were bursting to show us how good they were at the games. Kenneth got into the festivities by running around hitting everyone with the controllers. He didn't quite understand how it worked.

That afternoon and evening was given over to jumping, leaning, hula-hooping and insanity in all its glorious forms. Kenneth in particular loved the ski jump portion of Wii Fit (an exercise game). If the player fails to jump properly at the end of the ramp, he will roll down the hill in a giant snowball: arms, head, and skis poking out at various angles. Whenever he fell, which was often, he screamed in delight at the 'human snowball'.

The boys like to play baseball against each other on Wii Sports. Suffice it to say Alex usually gets the better of these games. One time though, Kiff simply trounced his older brother. After the three inning game Kiff led 4-2 and Alex was so frustrated he could hardly speak. What neither of them knew was I had given the baby a controller with no batteries. I held the operative one and had secretly 'helped'.

Mackenzie on the other hand is far too suspicious for such shenanigans on my part. Her favorite game is bowling, at which she is very good. Often her scores break 200 without much effort. I attempted to give Kiff a boost but missed my timing. His ball hurtled down the lane for a strike seconds before he had even moved.

I know, I feel shame.

***

We live in California's Central Valley. With irrigation, our farms produce some of the finest foods in the world. If you have ever eaten table grapes, carrots, or almonds then chances are they grew right here. In fact, I work in Wasco, Ca, the *Rose Capital of the World*. Some days you can hardly breathe for the waves of perfume wafting in from the fields.

Outside of Bakersfield we have large tracts of undeveloped hillside. During the brief spring rains (also known as April 20th) those mini-mountains will burst forth in violent, almost garish profusion of wild California Poppies.

Whenever possible the Eddy's will drive up into those lush vales and drink in the almost unheard of beauty. When you live in a desert, this type of green can be overwhelming if you're not careful.

A couple years ago we had rain for almost a week solid. This was unheard of and I knew the flowers would be glorious. That Saturday I packed-up the family and we made a day trip out into the hills. My heart aches for such an afternoon. We walked all over, taking pictures and immersing ourselves in nature. The tropical-green grass was soft and fragrant as we lay in the sun. The kids ran about like loons as if they would never tire. Heather and I strolled hand-in-hand, and fell in love all over again. It was Heaven.

Even when the kids ran up and pelted us with flower balls we just laughed for joy. I did have to put my foot down when they wanted to pick all the blooms and take them home in order to build a flower man in our front yard.

***

Alex and Mackenzie have brought an irritating little game into our family. While in the car they keep a close watch for VW Beetles. The first person to see one screams "BUG!" and punches everyone else in the arm. Needless to say, I am not crazy about my two teens punching each other as that often leads to weapons and unrestrained homicide. Nor do I particularly care for them punching me while I'm trying to hold onto the wheel cruising at 80 mph.

This has become so ingrained in them that Alex even whacked me while I was both driving and yelling at him for not doing his homework. Somehow he doesn't understand that hitting an already angry father is not one of the smartest things to do.

So last night we turn into the Costco parking lot (a veritable cornucopia of bug opportunity) when Kenneth slaps me in the back of the head and yells, "I'm bugging you!"

Why yes, yes you are.

***

Not all Kiff stories are funny. Occasionally his adventures simply break my heart. Yesterday our weekly visitation with Alex and Mack was coming to a close. Sunday at 6:00 p.m. their mother would arrive to once again take them away. These last few minutes of being a real family are usually punctuated with hugs and kisses, and sometimes tears. Kiff was in his room when he saw the pair of them walking out the front door. He took the most direct route of contact by leaping into his bedroom window and leaning against the screen.

Goodbye Alex. Goodbye Kinzie."

"Bye Kiff. We love you."

"I love you too."

The sadness in his voice cut me to the heart.

Then he yelled, "Alex's Mother! Are you going to bring them back tomorrow?"

"No," she replied, "They are going home with me until Thursday. And quit leaning on that window. You're gonna fall out."

"No! Please bring them back tomorrow so they can stay the night with me."

I can't blame her for dropping the conversation. What do you say to a five-year-old who is pleading for his brother and sister to stay?

"You're gonna bring them back tomorrow right? So they can stay the night with me?"

A few moments of silence passed as they retreated to their car.

"Okay, you bring them back tomorrow so they can stay the night." My eyes began to water.

At this point her other son, who is a mere 5 months older than Kiff, couldn't take the strain. He loves them just as much and missed them while they were away. In his bravest big-boy voice Ben called back, "No! They are going with me because they are *my* brother and sister!"

And from the depths of Kenneth's simplistic moral center came the answer, "You're evil for not letting me have them."

And so the tree of my poor choices continues to bear bitter fruit.

***

We're just your average family.
Brian as Henry VIII. Heather- the Queen who didn't lose her head over him. Alex the Zombie Hockey Player. Mack-'50s Poodle Skirt Girl. Kenneth was a Kung Fu Master.
*Ungeheuerlische Kinder- (German meaning "monsterlike children").

Chapter 5
Baby-In-A-Basket

I'm not quite sure what Kiff's thing is about worming into small places. Freud might say it was a desperate desire to return to the womb. Nietzsche would describe it in terms of alienation and fear of the outside world. Personally, I think he's more like a trapdoor spider, hiding out until he gets a good chance to strike.

***

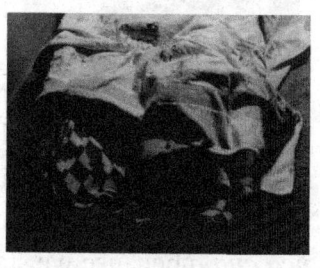

Who hasn't owned a pop-up hamper at some point? You know those cheap wire-and-mesh contraptions that supposedly can be folded down into a pot-holder sized circle when not in use. Most of the time they get bent into unrecognizable modern art and sit idle in the laundry room until someone throws it away in a fit of righteous indignation.

In our home, however, they serve just one purpose: a portable headquarters for the baby. From the moment he could crawl, Kenneth lived in those hampers. He would drag them from room to room and settle himself inside. Not just for naps mind you. He would play games, read books, watch TV, and eat his dinner from within the comfy confines of those netted-frames.

On days when (I can only assume) he felt especially vulnerable, he covered the hamper with a blanket before climbing inside. Like a Marine in his Ghillie Suit, Kiff would hide patiently for the unwary passer-by and then lunge out to trip them or gnaw on their ankles. This depending upon how long it had been since dinner.

**

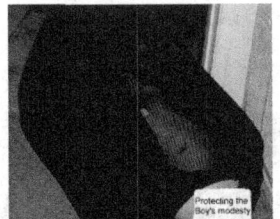

Though to us essentially the same thing as a pop-up hamper, Kiff had a very different purpose for the regular plastic laundry basket. This item served him as wheel barrel and occasional bed. And I must add a *mea culpa* because we started the whole business.

Heather and I lived in an apartment when Kiff was born. An apartment furthermore that had no laundry hook-ups. We had to walk a fair distance, up and down several flights of stairs, in order to do laundry. While he was young we could simply carry him in the basket with the rest of the damp and stinky items.

When the clothes were dry he would again hitch a ride in the basket but now cuddled by a mass of warm soft towels. No wonder he simply loved to be in the hamper. By the time he was big enough to walk, it was too late. The habit was already formed.

With a kid so enamored of sleeping in baskets and bins, you might think beds would be perfectly safe. In this you would be mistaken. Just as a cat simply 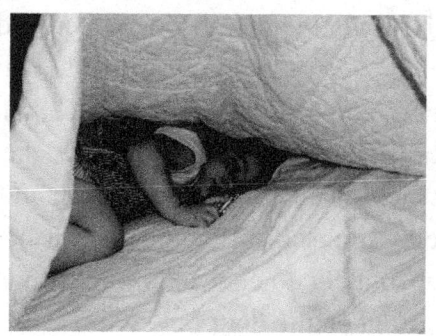 *must* walk across a patch of fresh concrete, Kenneth absolutely abhorred the sight of a neat and tidy bed.

The average life expectancy of a smooth coverlet was about 30 seconds. I swear to you Kenneth would sit quietly in his own room, watching Heather make the bed through his doorway. The instant she walked out he was all up in her business. He would play with toys under the cover, jump up and down and finally strip it completely.

His persistence finally beat our desire for order. We didn't have a nice looking bedroom for years.

***

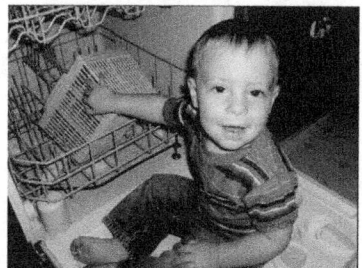 Growing up in the '70s, Heather and I got all the horror stories about kids being trapped inside abandoned freezers or falling into clothes dryers. We, like almost everyone else to whom this didn't

happened, quietly assumed that the parents were idiots. That would *never* happen to *my* kid. Oh how wrong…

Even before learning to crawl, Kiff learned to climb. We didn't fret too much when he got on to a chair or the couch. But I had to draw the line a few months later when I walked into the kitchen and found him trying to close himself inside the dishwasher! Granted there was absolutely no chance of him lifting his own weight while sitting on the door but still.

He played on that dish washer for almost a year. I can even place the event which made it stop. He climbed on one day and the screws holding it in place came loose. The whole washer tilted forward a few inches and partially closed on him. He didn't like that one bit and never tried to get up there again.

***

A whole book would not suffice to share all the stories about Kiff and his hiding places. So I will just share another 6000 words worth of pictures.

Chapter 6

The Pah-Tay

Our family isn't really into bathroom humor but (hee hee I said butt) this chapter just screams for it. So forgive me if things get a little unpleasant. I'll try to warn you beforehand. Because of our work schedules, Heather gets to spend much more quality time with Kenneth, particularly in the mornings. This has naturally resulted in her shouldering the lion's share of toilet duties (wah-ha-ha dooties). Therefore she will be telling many of these stories…

***

I won't bore you with the normal fiascos about changing diapers in the middle of the night; getting hit by the child's 'super soaker'; or even various accidents in public places. These are all very common with every infant and Bill Cosby told those tales long before this generation of Eddy's was even born. I just want to share one event which exemplifies the entirety of Kiff's diaper wearing life.

Kenneth has very sensitive skin. If his diaper was not changed within minutes of him doing business the entire area would become flaming red  and swollen. As a result, we often had to lie him on his favorite blanket in the living room, naked as a jay bird and looking somewhat like a baboon. Needless to say his mother and I were embarrassed anytime it happened and applied liberal amounts of rash medicine. This made it look like badly mixed strawberries-and-cream.

One evening, or rather early early one morning, I was changing the kid and found him red and raw. It was obvious he was in great discomfort and to make matters worse, we were out of cream. There was no way I was going to allow my son to suffer like that until morning. So like any good dad I packed him up and trooped off to Walgreens.

At 2:30 in the morning one is not always in their best state of mind. I believe this applies to both the desperate customer and the bored night clerk. When I walked in carrying a wailing infant wearing no diaper (the baby-I'm not back in diapers yet) the clerk knew exactly what I needed.

I assume she meant well but yelling down the aisle after me that what I really wanted was the 'Butt Paste' did not ease my sense of shame. A surprisingly large number of customers all pointed and stared at the zombie dad with his mismatched slippers and mad scientist hair, the baby lighting his path like some bass-ackwards Rudolph.

I shuffled to the counter and quietly lay down the tube of butt paste she had recommended. From that moment on I swear the situation was straight from one of those gross-out comedies. Women started jabbering about how I needed to take better care of my son. Why he was there at that time I don't know but some other toddler began to make retching sounds saying, "ooh yucky". The clerk had to get on the PA and ask the price of the Butt Paste because the register wasn't working right.

For a second I just knew Kiff was going to go for the trifecta and pee all over the counter. Luckily he didn't. No, he waited until I was putting him back in his car seat before blasting me. The night was perfect.

***

(Heather)...Kenneth is being potty-trained, too. If his diaper is off, he goes just fine. If it's on - no way, Jose. I've taken to bribery. It started out with a Hot Wheels car if he went potty [pee-pee] in the toilet. After he got good at that (and started asking for a car every five minutes) we switched to doing the other business for a car and getting a treat for going potty. Yesterday, he got the fifth and last car of the set of HW that I'd gotten for the bribing. He announced to me "You need to get more cars at Wal-Mart!" I have a feeling I've been had. He KNOWS how to go, but only if he's nekkid. It's cute - he says "My pee-pee is full" or his bottom is full. I don't know, maybe it's only cute to the mom and gross to everyone else. Too bad.

***

We've been very careful to make sure Kiff goes before hitting the sack. I am proud to say that his bed wetting has been almost nil. Only two or three occasions and we haven't even had to buy rubber sheets or pants. This has led to a few interesting late night conversations though:

"Kenneth, go potty!"

"Oh, not again!"

"Yes again. It tends to happen whenever you drink or eat."

"Not if I tell my pee-pee not to."

"Good luck with that."

***

An overheard conversation between Kenneth and himself in the bathroom:

"It's aliiiiive!"

"Kenneth! What's alive?"

61

"The meatloaf."

Uh…

***

WARNING…ICKY PART

Kids don't naturally know how to use toilet paper and lack much technique until they have practiced for a while. The high honor fell to yours truly when it came to making sure the kid was hygienic.

The setting: A man is sitting comfortably on his couch, sipping a cold drink and just opening the newspaper. As he begins to read a very interesting article about corruption in the local government he hears…

"Daaaaaaaaaaaaaaaaad, I'm done."

Bowing to his fatherly responsibilities he clambers to his feet and wends his way carefully through the toy-strewn house. He turns a corner into the bathroom and finds his youngest waiting for him.

"Daddy, I'm done."

He is stunned gazing on a two-year-old boy, hands, feet and head all firmly on the floor and backside lifted high in the air like a giant dung beetle, complete with dung.

The things we do for our kids.

Chapter 7
Mother's Milk

Oh how wonderful that connection between mother and infant. To bring forth life from one's own body, nurture and protect it. Grand is the joy to be felt in nursing a child, giving him food, comfort and love. How beautiful the tender mercies of motherhood.

My dear Heather only enjoyed this experience for a few short months. The whole time we feared he was not getting the nourishment he needed. Remember, Sir Urps-a-lot. That monster, post-partum depression, whispered that her milk was bad. Surely Kenneth was starving. We had to do something! I wasn't convinced all was lost but when Heather received a jury summons and simply could not be there to nurse, we agreed to try him on formula.

He took to it tolerably well but the vomiting did not slacken. He needed something else. There must be a special brand for picky eaters like our boy. We tried all the varieties without any improvement. In time though, we hit on the perfect substitute. One which was readily available at any grocery or convenience store: Diet Pepsi.

Precisely when Heather first gave him the elixir is not known. I do recall with some accuracy the first time he pulled himself up to a standing position. He'd crawled to the coffee table and strained higher and higher until ten pudgy little fingers grasped the edge. Then ever so slowly he rose onto his knees and finally onto those cute little biscuit feet. Immediately he lunged for the white foam cup before his eyes. I naturally assumed this was because of the high contrast of the white against a darker background, undeveloped eyes and all that. Heather jerked the cup from his grasp and we laughed a little. I should have taken the clue.

***

There comes a time in every child's life when she begins to vocalize her opinions. While little Timmy might *never* have liked strained peas, one day he will start yelling 'no' or 'yuck' before throwing the nasty mess on the floor. Kenneth is no exception.

At Church one bright and sunny Sabbath it came time to celebrate The Sacrament in memoriam of Christ's Last Supper. Rather than wine or grape juice, we employ plain water. When the time came for Kiff to partake he turned his face away, pushed back at the cup and then loudly proclaimed, "No! I want Diet Pepsi!" More than one head turned in our direction.

Understand my situation by remembering that, as a general rule, Mormons don't drink caffeinated sodas. I feel shame.

***

Recently the boy has begun creating his own food recipes. For example:

Rock Soup

1 package Oreo cookies
1 handful soda crackers
6 wands licorice
1 handful marbles
1 bottle secret ingredient

Directions:

Crush the Oreos into crumbs and drop into pot. Do same with crackers. Stir in licorice.

Drop in marbles from standing position so they stick into the mixture.

Last, add the bottle of secret ingredient, also known as Diet Pepsi.

Mix well and eat from pot.

He was beginning to make this for dinner when I wandered into the kitchen. Luckily he wasn't past the Oreo step and so I was able to convert it to a Rocky Road and Oreo sundae. He did have everything else spread out on the floor though. If I had not been craving ice cream at that instant he would have gone all the way.

***

Heather and I talked about how the child first tasted Diet Pepsi. Giving her the benefit of the doubt, it looks as though she absent-mindedly slipped him a straw full as an infant because well…he asked for it. I can't really blame her. Alex caught me a few weeks ago when he asked for a slice of cake…AT 11:30 IN THE EVENING!!!

"Go on, you know where it is", I mumbled in response.

Before I knew what had happened he was back with a mixing bowl full of frosted goodness and pigging-out contentedly.

***

Kenneth is still at the age where things like germs, strangers and individual property rights just don't exist. Neither at home nor in public is an unattended drink safe from the little hooligan's parched throat and probing fingers.

I should explain that last one. His Aunt Frankie (my brother's wife) likes to chew on ice. As his babysitter, the two of them watch movies and chomp down on a bucket-full of frozen crunch. Maybe it's a learned habit because my mother was famous for eating cups of salted ice. I never did it myself. Though now that I think about it…

So now Kenneth will not only drink from any cup he comes across, if the liquid is all gone he will fish out any bits of ice left. A most common event in our home runs something like this:

"Kenneth, leave my drink alone. Go get one for yourself."

Two minutes later the sound of a cup on the table brings me out of my book.

"Kenneth, don't drink my root beer. That's mine not yours."

The sound of the last drops of soda being slurped through a straw and rattling ice break the silence.

A dejected father whines, "Kiff that was the last of my root beer."

"Good. I didn't want that at all. Now we can have Diet Pepsi."

"But I don't like Diet Pepsi."

"Then can I have yours?"

***

Don't ask me why because I have no idea. About a year ago though, Heather decided she was going to wean the boy off that devil juice. This was not a good idea.

Aside from the constant whining, Kenneth began to search the house for those precious silver bottles. Our kitchen, at least those parts below the three foot line, was in constant chaos. Cupboards were disengorged of their contents. Cabinet doors flung open. The pantry was forever riffled to the bottom. 'No stone left unturned' was not too far from the truth. What he never discovered was that Mommy was hiding her stash atop the refrigerator where the young searcher could neither see, nor retrieve, the objects of his affection.

***

The Eddy's are not rich. To borrow a phrase, 'we have sufficient for our needs'. Of course, sometimes we like to go out to eat and if the money supply is plentiful at the moment we have been known to frequent restaurants where flip-flops are not the dress *de rigueur*.

Heather, Kenneth and I sat in the middle of a large and enthusiastic crowd. The tables were a bit cozier than I enjoy and more than once I had to apologize for nudging the kind older gentleman behind me. The atmosphere was so nice I failed to maintain my normal close watch on the boy. One moment he was there, the next he was not.

I didn't panic. In a very nonchalant way I thrust my head under the table cloth just in time to see Kiff's shoes disappearing out the other side. I sat up and looked around just as he reached the most forbidding couple in the room. Kenneth reached for the man's glass and I could just hear him say, "Is that Diet Pepsi? I like Diet Pepsi. Mommy said I couldn't have Diet Pepsi because Daddy said no but I would like some Diet Pepsi. Can I have some of your Diet Pepsi?"

I wonder if Kiff would have liked that Rum and Coke as much as Diet Pepsi?

***

There are endless stories of Kiff stealing Diet Pepsi. Sometimes he loses. Usually he wins. But one time he did both.

Because mom can reliably be expected to buy that succulent nectar, Kiff will set his sights on her cup first. Only if she catches him will he make alternate plans. One very warm summer's day he made a swipe at Mommy's tumbler. He didn't notice I had switched cups on him. It reached his mouth just as I yelled.

"Kiff! Stop drinking my root beer."

His tiny swollen face turned slowly toward me, cheeks puffed out with soda like a scavenging squirrel. Evidently the taste of the root beer was beginning to hit him and was not to his liking tonight, thank you very much.

His eyes began to water with fear and disappointment. Terrible sadness, perhaps even regret shone about his features. I almost began to feel sorry for him, until he leaned over my cup and spat it back in with a loud, "Yeeecch."

Little punk

***

Not too long ago I purchased the equipment for making soda at home. It is quite easy. Look it up on the internet.

When I told him what all the tanks and hoses were for he got *very* excited.

"Now you can make me Diet Pepsi at home and we won't have to buy it at the store."

70

"Yes Kenneth, I will be able to make you diet cola…"

"No NO NO NO! Daddy you're wrong. It's called Di-et Pep-si."

"Kenneth, diet means it has no sugar in it and Pepsi is a brand like Oreo or Gatorade."

"Oh Gatorade…put it in the G-series!"

Too much TV.

***

Sometimes you just have to ask the child what he is thinking.

"Kenneth, what is it about Diet Pepsi you like so much?"

"Oh…I luuuuuve Diet Pepsi. The bubbles tickle my nose and make me remember how much I love mommy for giving me Diet Pepsi."

Can't argue with that.

Chapter 8
Pink Pink You Stink

The child loves his toys of course. Today he clings to all the normal boy type playthings. But it wasn't always that way.

***

At birth, Kenneth was given a wide array of stuffed animals to gum on. By far the favorite came from a co-worker of mine named Sandy. She thought a George deserved a stuffed monkey far larger than himself.

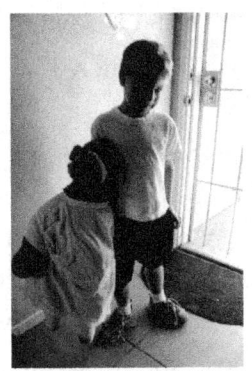

Soon the doll became the brother he always wanted. They even dressed alike much of the time.

***

Almost as soon as he could crawl, Kenneth began to steal Mackenzie's stuff. He raided her possessions with military precision and seemed to know exactly what he was after. One item in particular he prized above all others: her neon pink stuffed bear.

The beast came to live with us when Mack refused to let me donate it for a Teddy Bear Toss at the Hockey game. She loved on it for years before Kiff came around. Soon the two children were engaged in all-out war over who was going to own the hideous monstrosity. I'll tell you how Kiff finally won.

One bright spring day the boy kidnapped Pink Bear and smuggled it over to the sitter's house. Free of interference, he worked on it all day long. By the time I arrived (Alex and Mack in tow) to bring Kenneth home, the bear was sopping with vomit and drool.

Mack took one look at the bedraggled mess, heaved a groan of disgusted surrender and sighed, "You keep it Kiff. It's soooo grooooooossssssss."

The toothless grin she got back may have been thanks or victorious mockery. We'll probably never know.

***

Pink Bear is not the only one of his off-color knickknacks. He also has a pink giraffe, a pink snake and for good measure a small electric green spider monkey which still gives Heather nightmares. These of course live in the Kiff Zoo along with Blue Bear, Brown Bear and the 101 Happy Meal toys from Mickey D's.

***

Don't get me wrong, Kiff has a whole slew of toys beside stuffed animals. There are blocks of every shape and size. The tinker toys, cars, books, beads, crayons, sports equipment and action figures form a thin crust over his bedroom floor. He has discovered scissors and what wonderful shapes they can make. And don't get me started on the 10,000 marbles scattered loosely throughout the house. "Clean your room" is less a daily chore than the concerted assault on an implacable foe.

We parents have come to an uneasy truce with the boy. So long as the mess is confined to his room, we will only scream once a week. When it inches down the hall and into the rest of the house like The Blob had formed inside a Toys-R-Us, then we have to put our foot down (if there is any space). It is then we call upon Gunny Bag.

***

Contrary to what my friends and family may think, I do listen to the advice of others. Nestled within a "mommy blog" was the answer to our toy tidal-wave problem. The enterprising woman sewed a very large sturdy bag and dropped into it any toy which was not in its place. On Saturday, Gunny Bag would return from Mom's room and give back all the toys. I thought this was wonderful. Kiff thought it a load of horsepucky.

I acquired a cavernous canvas bag (say *that* five times fast) and that night we introduced it to Kenneth. No tortured banshee could cry and wail like our sweet little popkin did when Pink Bear leapt into the bag followed quickly by a dozen Hot Wheels cars, two books, a hockey stick and the broken remains of a bobblehead which he had decapitated just to see how it worked.

"Now Kenneth, Gunny Bag will come every night and eat any toys which are left out. But he will be back on Saturday so you can have them again."

He looked at the bag. He looked at us. Again he looked at the bog. Once more he looked at us. Then in a voice like Dirty Harry he said, "I will kill Gunny Bag."

During that week I filled the bag with almost every toy the child owned. It stood five feet tall and three around with odd lumps and jagged corners sticking out all over. Every night before bed Kiff would enter our room, kneel down before Gunny Bag and say his prayers which usually sounded something like this:

"Dear Heavenly Father. Thank you for this day. Please bless Mommy and Daddy. Please make Gunny Bag throw-up all my toys and then go away and die. Amen."

Despite our pain at seeing the boy's distress, we stuck to our guns. For the next three weeks we dutifully filled the bag and emptied it again. But the terror of Gunny Bag seemed to wear off.

His first act of defiance was to tip the bag on its side and rescue one of his prized possessions from the evil monster. Soon, it wasn't enough to burgle what he could and flee. At least three times I found my room flooded with plastic doo-dads because he had managed to pull the bag over and pour everything out. Of course that made the pickins easier and shows a bit of wisdom. If you are going to steal things back from dad, better make sure they are worth the punishment.

By the time Gunny Bag was a fortnight old, Kiff was getting serious. I heard the telltale crash of toys falling to the floor and rushed to my room where, I swear to you, Kenneth had climbed bodily inside the bag and was kicking his treasures out.

It was like some terribly cheap horror movie from the '60s. This huge tubular mass, writhing and undulating on the ground, spitting out the remains of whatever toys were held by the dozen or so children it had consumed hours before. If I hadn't been laughing so hard, I would have been sick.

Eventually we abandoned Gunny Bag. Once all his toys were gone he just amped up the imagination and started playing with shadows on the wall or power tools. You know, whatever he could get his hands on (just kidding).

***

Kenneth has a small but interesting collection of bath toys. This motley crew consists of a couple boats, some old glow sticks, a cup for pouring and a water-proof book. He loves these toys but above them all are the Ducks.

As you can see, his coterie is a well-disciplined group. After every bath they form a straight line and await inspection by the sergeant-at-arms. Am I wrong to fear a touch of OCD in the kid? His mom and dad sink into the madness occasionally.

***

And speaking of lining things up obsessively... Kenneth likes to connect stuff. Any two objects will do and no medium is unusable. I have watched him tear out long strips of cellophane tape just so he could tack one end to the refrigerator and the other to the couch. He will meticulously arrange hundreds of tiny beads from his room, going 20 feet down the hall and into the living room, just so he can match his bed to the TV. The only rule is that the line cannot, *must not*, be broken. Any messing with the line is cause for a titanic tantrum. Not that we allow that to continue for long.

***

Elsewhere I mention that Heather gets to spend a bit more time alone with Kenneth than I do. They are together in the mornings after I go to work and stay up later at night. Therefore she gets to see more of his, uniqueness, than I do.

Our family was sitting down for pizza at Costco when Heather casually said, "Later I'll tell you where Kenneth was putting the beads last night."

I gave her a quizzical look.

"It's not appropriate for dinner time."

That brought to mind several mental images from comical to downright unpleasant.

I confess to being a bit let down when she told me he had tried to stuff his nose. If finger lasers can go in, why not a simple bead?

***

One of the child's favorite toys is a set of over-sized blocks Grampa Eddy gave him. Left to his own devices, Kiff will build the most fantastic creations: huge palaces with hot and cold running Diet Pepsi; airports for all the people who want to come be his friend; race tracks where he and Lightning McQueen try to win the Piston Cup; and many mini machines. These industrial engineering brainwaves are usually in response to something Heather or I have done. Like all good techno-geeks, Kiff believes any problem can be solved by building a better machine.

The process goes something like this:

"Kenneth, I don't want you talking to your mother like that. She is an adult and a good person and deserves your respect."

"Daddy, I'm gonna build a machine that gives Mommy all the respect she needs so I don't have to give her any."

Come to think of it, I'd like one of those.

Chapter 9
Isn't Everything Clean at the House of Mouse?

I LOVE DISNEY. I love it, I love it, I love it. Ever since I was a little child the whole Disney mystique has held me spellbound. As a teenager at Disneyland I would study the maps until absolutely nothing was beyond my keen. If you wanted to know the quickest route to a drinking fountain or Frontierland or the emergency medical station, I could tell you. My greatest ambition is to restore the apartment located above *Pirates of the Caribbean* and live inside the park. I have collected, expanded and written a series of origin stories for each of the ghosts in the *Haunted Mansion*. We search for Hidden Mickeys in the park. Heck, when I get serious about a woman, the first thing I do is take her to Disneyland to find out how much fun she *really* is. Not to mention I do a pretty darn good Goofy impersonation.

Naturally then, we go to Anaheim as often as money permits. The last couple years Heather and I have made it a bit of a Christmas tradition. When Kiff was almost four we decided it was time to indoctrinate…er introduce him…to the Wonderful World of Disney.

The original park and California Adventure share an adjoining congregatium where the sheeple can be penned until opening. The name C.A. is spelled out in large letters before the gates and I am sure countless visitors have created digital memories hanging on those structures. We certainly did. Kenneth wanted to climb up on Mickey's shoulders but I thought security  would throw us out. And at $90 a ticket, I wasn't going anywhere but inside. He settled for a picture of him with his brother and sister. Ain't they cute?

Disneyland proper lies beyond the turnstiles and a small entrance walk where one can get a very nice view of the D.L. Railroad (a personal favorite). Kiff became very excited and for a short time he ran about imitating a train. It would probably have lasted all day had not endless wonders lay within. His first real look at the magic though happened after we passed through the tunnels and entered Main Street USA.

None of the others had ever been to the park during the Holidays and, as I hoped, our trip proved spectacular. This was, as I said, the Christmas Season and so a traditional tree stood in the Main Street Plaza. Alex in particular was in awe of the gigantic, perfectly decorated spruce which rose 800 feet into the cool

December air. Well, maybe it wasn't quite 800 feet. But it sure looked like it to him.

***

Surprisingly, Kenneth behaved exactly the way one might expect a four-year-old to while visiting the Magic Kingdom. He ran about like a loon on meth. Everything had to be touched. All the food required tasting by his expert lips. "How did they do that?" and "Why can't I go on that?" were the most frequently uttered phrases. Actually, some variation of "No, Kenneth" was constantly hanging in the air.

You would think a kid like Kiff in Fantasyland would produce stories to fill this whole book. But he just didn't do anything all that crazy. Granted, worming his way through the crowd barricades so that his leash was knitted throughout was amusing. And my heart raced a bit when he tried to climb out on the slopes of the rock formation of Tom Sawyer's Island (don't give me any of this *Pirate Island* crap or whatever they're calling it these days). The fact is, there is only one good story from that trip and it still makes me squeamish.

***

Child psychologists say there are definite stages to youth development, one of which is oral. That is to say, the kid either eats or licks everything. We caught the tail end of his oral fixation while at the park.

I'm glad Disney doesn't swab for DNA because every surface they check for the next year is gonna have Kenneth spit on it. I caught him licking the chains meant to keep us in line. He sucked on all the silverware at the table when we had lunch. He tried to bite-off Mickey's fingers. Suffice to say, if it was within tonguing distance, he slathered it.

Heather and I tried. We really tried. But the child has the lingual dexterity of a bull frog. You'd think he was out of range but suddenly tttthhhhpppppttttt. We were reduced to holding our hands over his mouth but then he would just drool all over us and laugh his horrible maniacal cackle.

Heather finally had enough when she, bringing-up the rear of our group, slid her hand across the rail and into a slimy snotty mass of Kiff muck. Her piercing scream made me think she had been attacked by Tinker Bell and the rest of the pixies. In a public park 200 miles from home, we couldn't give him the discipline he so richly deserved & apparently wanted. So we talked to him. And talked. And talked. Not one bit of it meant anything to him. Just after taking this picture, he tried to lick my camera lens.

***

Don't get me wrong though, Kenneth is not a perpetual motion machine. The evening wore on and he drooped just a little. I was carrying him on my shoulders a lot more which, believe me, did nothing good for my back.

About 10 p.m. the kid and I wandered into the Central Plaza just as a light show began at Cinderella's Castle. The display was impressive. Brilliant colors bathed it in blues and golds, burst out in purest white and then twinkled to reddish purple.

Kenneth raised a sleepy head, let out a soft exclamation of wonder and murmured, "Daddy, that's pretty." I managed to catch the moment on film.

Chapter 10
Cars Crash in Flat-Out II

Is it wrong to say every American boy in the last 50 years has had Hot Wheels or Matchbox cars? I certainly did. In fact my room routinely became a massive stunt show with tracks running from ceiling to floor. I would make them turn circles on the linoleum; loop-the-loop around bed posts; and jump the sleeping cat. And there's nothing wrong with that. I never hit the animals (they were too fast).

Kenneth seems to love his cars just as much. We bought him a couple track sets and like every other boy in the world he assembled them carefully, ran the cars about 10 times and then took everything apart so he could make one long jump from the top of the bunk beds into a glass of water.

***

Eventually the long plastic tracks were forgotten. Little boys can only handle so much frustration and trying to figure out the physics of bridge trestles or the inclination of jump ramps is soooooo bothersome. Plus Mom and Dad never let you bring the darn things along when you go visit Grandma.

Soon a little canvas bag was stuffed with blocks, books and a half dozen cars. This would go everywhere with the kid and provide hours of fun and distraction.

Much to the relief of a certain pair of loving but worn-out parents

***

Remember in Chapter 8 when I mentioned his obsessive need to line things up? This picture might help you see what I meant. Notice the monopoly money all laid out neatly. Now look closer. Did you catch the pattern? One piece

crossways followed by two then another one etc. When I first espied this I was sure he had finally flipped-out. We were just dialing the child psychologist when he looked-up, smiled and said, "I built a race track because cars crash in Flat-Out two."

For the next several minutes he explained about the six racers and the pace car there on the far right. They were competing for the Piston Cup but Lightening McQueen wasn't racing because he was in Radiator Springs with Doc and Mater.

***

Something about that phrase caught my attention though. "Cars crash in Flat-Out two". It was odd.

Certainly cars crash and to a five-year-old that is very amusing. Come to think of it, some adults would agree as long as they don't own or ride in the car. But what did he mean by 'Flat-Out two'?

I didn't have to wonder for long. The next day I collected the kid from his sitter when he took me by the hand and walked to a computer near-by. There on the screen was a racing game: Flat-Out II. His cousin Julie was playing a weird bonus round of car bowling. She revved the engine until is whined like a jet and let off the brakes. It flew down the track to a ramp and launched through the air before crashing spectacularly among 10 massive bowling pins. She got a 7-10 split. Kenneth started rolling on the floor in hysterics.

I guess he was right. Cars *do* crash in Flat-Out II.

***

For six months, Kiff felt it was his Divine mission to let everyone know about the joy to be found in F-O II. No missionary could be more devout in spreading the good news. He would end every phone conversation with the proclamation. Strangers he met were soon informed. And even The Lord's infinite patience must have been tested after Kenneth loudly announced his message during prayers for 47 straight days.

***

Somewhere about this time I discovered the music of Rob Zombie. Okay, get all your gasps and groans out of the way. Once you move past the sheer *loudness* of it, he does write some evocative lyrics and the, I won't say melody, but power of the music is perfect for my Kung Fu workouts.

Imagine my surprise when Kenneth began not only to dance to but sing along with a piece called *Demon Speeding*.

"Kiff, where do you know this song from?"

"It's the Flat-Out II song!" he cried happily.

It's also a nice little dance number if you know, wanna kick-up your heels.*

From *The Mountie Song* by The Arrogant Worms off the album Live Bait.

Chapter 11
LodPig

In 1982 a skinny boy walked into the local Thrifty's Drug store and saw something amazing. There on display was a small black box about twice the size of a loaf of bread. It was connected to a television set and on the screen was a laughably simple game called River Raid. That boy was never the same.

Thirty years later, the man has seen those early Atari 2600 machines advance to PS3's and Kinects which wirelessly mimic your every action. The graphics are almost real to life and every conceivable type of game or adventure can be indulged in to the limits of human desire.

His sons are even more deeply addicted than he ever was.

***

DO DO, DA-do DA-do Pet-ville

About a year ago, Kenneth began telling me all about this pet he owned named LodPig. I assumed it was another in the long line of imaginary toys / pets / friends of which he was continually chattering. There was even a cute little song to go with it. He seemed happy and that made me happy.

After a few days however I heard an odd conversation between him and Heather.

"Mommy, I need to feed LodPig."

"No Kiff. I am using it right now."

"But Mommy, he's going to starve."

"He'll be fine for another hour."

Wondering what the heck they were talking about I moseyed into Heather's art / computer room and foolishly asked.

Kenneth then launched into a very long explanation about his pet and how it liked to wear dresses sometimes but usually not because it was a boy and that he could change how the pet looked but it always had to have 'Star Wars' eyes. He very unkindly added that Mommy "wanted his pet to die because she wouldn't let [him] feed LodPig".

Finally Heather patiently told me about the Facebook-based game Petville. For those who have never played it, the action is fairly simple. The player creates a pet from a large array of body types. They choose a house, furniture, toys and almost endless other amenities. They then take care of the pet. Over time the character gets dirty and needs to be washed. They get hungry and you must feed them. The better care one take of their pet, the more points awarded. Points are then used to buy more stuff. Other players on Facebook can visit your pet and even buy them things. Simple. It costs nothing but your time and attention.

Because of the social nature of the game, it helps to know as many other players as possible. This seems to be how Kiff got involved. Someone I know well but will not name *cough* Heather *cough* created an account for him so her own pet would have a friend.

For months Kiff was a very dedicated pet owner. He would tend to LodPig's needs with a level of tenderness surprising in a 5-year-old. The only complaint was his rampant consumerism.

The boy is a hoarder. He would buy four couches and twelve food bowls so his (I hesitate to say) dog could lie down or eat in any room it chose. Every other day Heather would have to go in and sell tons of junk just so we could see the animal on screen. Kiff thought this was very very funny.

I am sad to say LodPig is wandering somewhere in cyberspace, filthy and haggard. Kenneth has neglected him by not playing Petville in quite a while. The call of bigger and better games caught his attention.

***

I mentioned the Wii system earlier. We haven't allowed Kiff to manage it alone, changing discs or anything of that sort. But over time he has become rather adept at playing some of the games. Like many earlier systems, Nintendo likes to bundle several small titles onto one disc. One of those compilations is WiiSports.

Kenneth likes to golf. Rather I should say: Kenneth likes to target golf. Imagine a tee-off. One hundred yards away, floating in the middle of a lake, is a huge bull's-eye green. Another hundred yards away is a second green. Closest to the centers gives the most points. The boy is a natural duffer. Weird though, he likes to shoot at the closer target despite the lower scores

93

possible. He looks a bit like Bill Murray teeing off on the carnations from *Caddyshack*.

The boxing game is also a favorite of his. If enthusiasm were a true replacement for skill or coordination then I would be raising Kiff Ali. He gets so into the punches that more than once he has knocked himself down. Luckily he beat the standing eight-count.

Have you ever noticed the odd way some bowlers wiggle their butt just before approaching the lane? I have. It has something to do with setting their feet in the right position or giving full entertainment value to the audience. Anyway, Kiff goes through the whole routine before ever so gently lobbing his ball toward the pins. Half the time it goes forward and the other half backwards. Either way it flies twenty feet through the air before landing with a heavy thud on the floor. I've never seen anyone throw their ball back into the seats before but I am certain everyone would jump in panic just as they do in the game.

Like most good red-blooded American boys, Kenneth loves to play baseball. The Wii version is far simpler than say MLB2012 for the Xbox and that works just fine for my boy. He finds great enjoyment in striking me out. His older brother has taught him the finer points of trash talk. Just last week he beat me 3-1 and I was actually trying.

Rotten so-and-so.

**

Another of his favorite games is WiiFit+. This is a fitness program designed to help an individual focus on types of exercise disguised as fun activities. Say you wish to improve your balance. WF+ offers a Segway simulator where you chase balloons across a beach. Not your type of fun? How about what Kiff refers to as Marblehead? Huge marbles are dropped onto a free floating plate. The player leans around to tilt the plate and drop the marbles through a hole. Don't let them fall off the edge or a time penalty hits you as well as getting a replacement ball. Why Marblehead? The faces of different player characters are painted on the marbles. He loves to scream out, "I dropped you off the world Daddy!"

Fit Plus also has some jogging games for conditioning. The scenery is taken from a variety of Mario titles and is really quite lovely. Kenneth will run in place just as fast as he can to make his Mii fall over in a cloud of dust.

**

WiiPlay is another volume set. Kenneth likes to fish and play pool but the one he enjoys the most is Tanks. This game has the player face off with one or more enemies. You can fire your cannon in any direction or drop a mine which will explode after 15 seconds. He doesn't quite understand what he's supposed to do yet.

Blowing himself up with a bomb makes him laugh just as hard as getting the bad guy.

***

His current game facination is *Angry Birds*. For the longest time I refused to even find out what the game was. Call it the contrarian in me. Kenneth is infatuated with it. Aside from being quite good at killing pigs; Kiff sings about Angry Birds; talks about Angry Birds; decorated a t-shirt with Angry Birds and begs to play it every night. A couple weeks ago I let him play as much as he wanted on a lazy Saturday. Five hours later I could no longer stand the whoops of triumph each time a bird exploded.

***

The only other game which might come close is a new obsession called *Plants versus Zombies*. I don't know it very well but it must be fun. Kiff actually said, "I've killed enough pigs. Now I want to go kill zombies!" Every few minutes I hear him announce, "I got the cherry bomb!" or "I got the shovel". I wince each time I hear this because neither of these are very safe in the hands of a kindergartener.

Oy vey!

**

The line between video games and movies has become so blurred that my dear 5 year old is having difficulty distinguishing one from another. He currently is enthralled by the Tron movies, both of them.

Every aspect of his life now carries some reference to the films. He doesn't 'eat', he gains energy. People are not 'in charge', they are users. And above all, his desire to kill me is now expressed in the need for his father to be 'de-rezzed'.

This mania has grown to the point of moving outside our home. Last Sunday we were seated next to Sister Judy in church (you'll meet her in Chapter 17). She is obviously pregnant and Kenneth felt it was time to offer his wise counsel. Their conversation went something like this:

"Sister Judy, do you have a baby in your tummy?"

"Yes Kenneth, I do."

"What are you going to name the baby? Because I think you should name him Baby-Tron."

It is a tribute to her knowledge of sci-fi movies and sense of humor that she just smiled and said she'd think about it.

***

Kenneth is quite serious about his gaming. The petunias and eggplant were busy fighting off zombies while I watched old episodes of Star Trek: DS9. Kiff walked into the living room with a very disgusted look on his face.

"Daddy, I have some bad news for you. Your movie is distracting me and making me lose to the zombies."

"Oh, I am so sorry about that son. Do you know what we should do about that?"

"Uh…"

"I agree! We should turn off the computer and you should watch Star Trek with me."

For some reason he didn't like that solution very much.

Chapter 12
Everybody's Friend

Kenneth suffers from an excess of bravery. There is no danger he cannot overcome; noise he will not embrace; nor stranger with whom he will not go home. In all seriousness, Heather and I are a bit worried about that last one. Even as an infant he didn't mind being held by new people. Often times they would misunderstand his usual greeting of massive vomiting as a sign of nervousness. We in the family knew he was just baptizing them into his circle of friends.

***

The boy had an annoying (and provocative) habit of crawling underneath lady's dresses. Any chance he got the little rug rat would scamper past the hemline and then stand up to play in the "tent". He made a lot of friends that way.

***

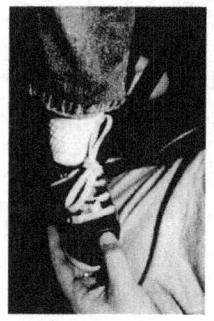 Once he began to walk we had a whole new set of concerns. If his hand was not firmly set into one of ours, off he went to find a new family to torture…er I mean share exciting new discoveries with. Our only solution has caused us no end of ridicule and stress…the leash.

I know child safety harnesses have been available for years and years. And my peace of mind is worth all those weird looks. But when a stranger in the store tried to say I should be turned into Child Protective Services for treating my child like a dog, I had to put my foot down. Kenneth is simply like no other child when it comes to the sheer joy of exploration.

If there weren't that slight time gap, I would swear he were Chris Columbus' kid. And I don't mean the guy who almost ruined the Harry Potter franchise with the first two movies.

***

 Like any good guerrilla fighter, Kiff quickly learned how to use this new restriction to his advantage. First he tried to make it as difficult as possible for me to use the leash. He would put the harness on backwards or surreptitiously get it tangled while I was tying his shoes.

Later he began to elicit sympathy from strangers, crying and tugging at the leash as if it were hurting him. The act was so utterly convincing he almost got a kiss from Tinker Bell while we sojourned at Disneyland because he seemed to be suffering so much.

Kenneth came off victorious in the war of wills over his leash. I must admit, my capitulation was entirely in the interest of self-preservation. I could stand the whining, tugging, twisting and even occasional bouts of dragging. But when he discovered a means of actually causing me bodily injury, I felt the game had gone too far.

During one of our excursions out into the badlands east of town, Kenneth became suspiciously cooperative. He walked at my side; didn't run off to explore the nearby gullies; heck, we offered to let him off the leash if he would behave. The child wanted none of it. Then just as we reached a point in the road where a sheer drop to the side combined with a steep grade to maximize the danger, he suddenly ran a loop around my ankles and pulled with all his might. I almost fell down the side of a mountain just after this picture was taken.

***

Entering school may have been a slight culture shock for Kiff. Never before has he had to go more than a few minutes without being the center of attention. Heather and I are not 'helicopter' parents who hover nearby breathlessly waiting for their little dictator's every demand. On the other hand, he is just so darned cute it's hard to ignore him for long.

According to Heather, the boy was adamantly against walking in line. Actually, he was fine with it…as long as he got to walk next to the teacher and hold her hand.

***

We have noticed a slightly worrisome trend about our little guy. While he will play with anyone or all by himself, he doesn't recognize when other kids don't want him around. This social blindness might make for some awkward times later if he doesn't learn to read other's behavior.

Some Mickey D's restaurants still have the large play areas. I took Kiff there for some Father / Son time a while back and things did not go well.

First a group of rowdy boys slightly larger than Kenneth began to push the little ones off the slides. Kenneth stood up and told them to be nice. They laughed in his face and said a few choice words even I had never heard before.

Kiff didn't get angry but kept following them around trying to play with the group. Eventually they left but this puppy dog act is most unsettling. We'll see how well he does the first time a kid takes a swing at him.

***

On the other hand, Kenneth can wrap adults around his little finger. He talked his mom into buying Panda Express for dinner. Kiff settled himself into a nearby booth while Heather got in line. Before she knew it, the child had struck-up a conversation with three 20-somethings at the next table. He told them all about Clock America (Ch. 20), his 16,000 super powers and the secret government program he was part of, which of course is why they had never heard of his super powers.

Heather began to play along and prompted him to introduce himself.

"Hello, my name is Kenneth Calvin George Eddy and what is your name? But you can call me Kiff. And what are the names of your charming lady friends?"

They had a sense of humor too because the guy answered, "My name is Robert and that is Stacy. You can't know her name because she is mine."

He thought that was very funny.

Chapter 13
Call the Fashion Police

Although no one in our family wears Armani or Gucci, neither are we to be found in tube tops and coveralls…usually. We try to look good most of the time. Kiff however has a love / hate relationship with clothes. Actually, he has a hate / hate relationship with 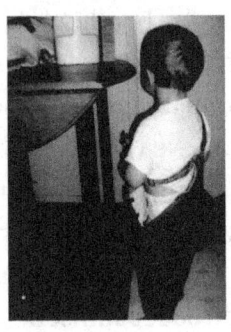 clothes. The following stories will hopefully show what I mean.

***

From the first moment Kiff could dress himself, he stubbornly put everything on backwards. To this day he wears his underwear and shirts front-to-back. I have tried and tried to correct him but he will have none of it.

 Not until a year later was I finally given an explanation: He's giving the tags a "tummyback" ride.

***

My Brother's Knickers

At four years old Kenneth began to have opinions about what he was going to wear. Generally we have put our metaphorical feet down in the day time, but at night the kid has a bit more leeway. The only things we demand are clean underwear and some type of covering shirt. If he wants to wear mismatched socks, holey sweats or over-sized hockey shirts, well, who's getting hurt right? The underwear is a continual problem. He simply does not want to have his bottom covered. That Gluteus Minimus appears to be a point of pride with the kid and he takes every opportunity to show it to anyone who will look. I fear for the community at large when he realizes that teenagers sometimes "moon" for fun. Kenneth is going to be the first person picked out of a police butt line-up.

***

Inexplicably he not only put on some skivvies without being told tonight, but was very proud of himself.

"Daddy, I'm wearing my brother's underwear!" he announced loudly.

I turned to find him with a Condors hockey jersey pulled up over his head and a pair of shorts six sizes too large around his narrow hips. I chuckled lightly and sent him off to see his mother.

"Mommy! I'm wearing my brother's underwear!"

"Those don't fit you. Go take them off right now."

Kenneth thinks she's a party pooper. I think she wanted to see if he would trip on the cotton bag which hung down below his knees.

**

Very far back in our family history there sleep a few Teutonic ancestors. They came from southern Bavaria and made highly dubious claims to royalty. Kiff seems to be channeling their spirits by slipping into my over-the-calf tube socks like a pair of lederhosen.

**

I made the distinction between day and evening wear. Bedtime is another matter completely. In winter he will usually allow us to put him in PJs or even footies. During our hot summers he strips down to skivvies or just a toga if he can get away with it. I think he's almost ready for college now.

**

Like most boys, Kenneth went through a phase where he didn't mind being dressed up in his sister's clothes. We took it stoically and my own sister reminded me of a terrible month when I was 'Brianna'. But we don't talk about that.

The worst however was when he discovered mommy's bra. For several weeks he demanded she put it on him.

"I have boobies!" he would proudly announce.

I blame her for confusing his sexual personae.

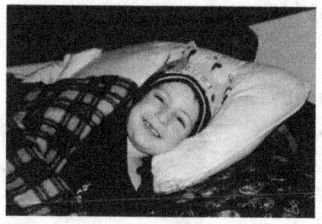 The whole clothes thing must be an offshoot of the OCD. He will fixate on one thing for months at a time and then just as suddenly forget it ever happened.

We made a very rare trip to a burger place that does not sell Happy Meals. As I recall it was on a trip to the small mountain village of Tehachapi. They grow apples there. We stopped into the King's place and Kenneth got his very first crown. We couldn't get the darned thing off his head for days. It finally disappeared after he tried to wash it in the bath.

***

The second *Austin Powers* movie featured a character named Mini-Me. He was the exact clone of Dr. Evil except 1/6 his size. Imagine the shock I felt when my own mini-me walked out of the bedroom one night. Kenneth had donned one of my work shirts, a pair of my jeans, and slipped into my tall work boots which rose to mid-thigh. Then he stumped around like a two foot tall lumber jack saying, "I'm my daddy. Fuh fuh fuh."

Chapter 14
The Littlest Dragon

Some people have hobbies.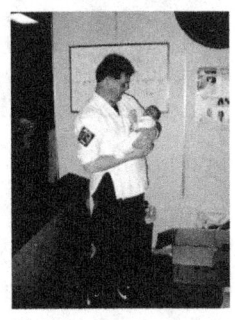
Others have obsessions. Amateurs
say I. For the better part of 16 years
I invested a major portion of my
time, blood, sweat and tears into
studying Martial Arts. Specifically a
style called *Toi Li Ho Fut Hung* or
in America *Kung Fu San Soo*.

Developed in ancient China and brought to the LA
area in the '30s, San Soo enjoys a small but devoted
following in Bakersfield. We have boasted up to four
studios operating at one time and are honored to claim no
fewer than 10 Masters (8th degree Black Belt). The Art
has been a huge part of my life.

When Kenneth was born, I took a few days off in
order to help Heather recuperate. It wasn't long before
she declared me a nuisance and sent me back to the

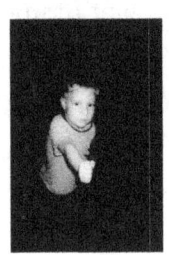 Fighting Dragons. At least there my ham-
handed antics and being under foot would
not be out of place. Naturally I took
Kenneth in to show him off.

For the next two years he dutifully
accompanied me twice a week and served
not only as a conversation piece but

occasionally as a prop. More than once I demonstrated various methods of one-handed fighting, the kid firmly in my arms. Proud to say I never dropped him, though once he did stop a punch for me. Just kidding.

Most of the time Kenneth sat in his portable play pen. I brought numerous toys and books for him. One guess as to what he did with them. That's right…the moment we began to spar he would cry and throw things at whomever was fighting me.

Speaking of that playpen, he never really liked being in there. At first he tried to climb the sides but wasn't quite tall enough. Then he began to burrow. He'd pry up the bottom pad at the corner and slip quietly underneath. Soon all the toys and books were neatly hidden as well. Eventually the child realized there was no tunnel to freedom so he took a more direct approach. Like a professional wrestler, he stood at one side and ran full speed at the other. There were no elastic ropes to spring him back so the whole pen tipped up onto two legs. Harder and harder he threw himself against the wall until finally he succeeded in knocking it over completely. He was a sight, sprawled out on the floor with all his toys tumbled out around him, a hard fierce look of triumph in his eyes.

***

Long before I wanted Kenneth grew tall enough to climb out of his playpen. I begged him to stay inside, to behave. We warned him dire things would happen if he left the safe place. My words fell on deaf ears.

Sure enough near tragedy struck. About 10 of us were free-styling (fighting at 90% speed with minimal contact) and so bodies were flying everywhere. Out onto the mats came my precious one, running to 'save' his daddy. Of course just at that moment I was thrown in his direction. Upside-down in mid-air I noticed the boy's frail little body in the exact spot I was destined to land. A quick twist and shove to the ground allowed me to bounce awkwardly to the side. I'm told it was an impressive bit of body control. Kenneth wasn't impressed. He got mad at me for scaring him.

***

That first little adventure didn't cure him of coming onto the mats either. For some reason which completely baffles me Kiff was fascinated with David, the studio owner. Now Dave is a fine man and an excellent fighter but not exactly the cuddly type. Perhaps it's because he is going prematurely bald. Rather than comb over, David took the plunge and started shaving his hair clean-off. It gives him a sinister look…unless he's flashing his boyish smile.

Just as soon as my boy could break free of the playpen, he was headed for the mats. I flatter myself to say he wanted to be with Daddy but that little fantasy soon melted away. Dave and I were working a ground

110

technique when Kenneth rushed up to us and began rubbing the poor confused guy's shiny noggin, all the while giggling like Kermit the Frog on helium.

I won that fight. Tag team points for the Eddy boys.

***

David built a really nice coffee table for the studio. It's a shallow two foot by five foot box on legs with a glass table-top. Inside he put 50 pounds of sand to make a Zen garden. I think he missed his calling as a carpenter.

Kenneth was forever sliding the glass to one side so he could run his fingers around and mess-up Dave's carefully sculpted lines. That is until he and his mother hit upon the idea to drop Star Wars action figures in to recreate the Sarlacc pit from *Return of the Jedi*.

***

My class of pre- to mid-teens needed to learn ways to recognize an attack and make evasive maneuvers. So I made a game of it. They ran in a large circle around the mats and I stood in the middle throwing things at them. If it were something soft like a plastic ball then they were supposed to block it away. Anything hard coming at them needed to be avoided.

Now don't criticize my method as a teacher. You have to understand the lesson before the technique makes any sense. The drill worked wonders not only for their ability to see objects quickly but also decision making. That is until Kenneth joined the fun.

Suddenly the drill was worthless as my little klepto kept running about stealing all the various balls, discs and knick-knacks I had been tossing around. He gathered them into a pile and growled at anyone who tried to come near.

***

Soon he became a sort of mascot for the studio. David very kindly allowed him a semi-official job as parent-sitter. While I taught lessons, Kiff performed amazing feats of daring-do for the delight of any adult who happened to be hanging out.

His show consisted mainly of walking atop the four inch wide barrier separating the workout floor from the entry way. When not improving his balance, the child was equally likely to use his audience as a climbing wall. More than one girl commented that ten minutes with Kenneth was like two hours at the drive-in with a very touchy-feely date.

My Boy!

***

Life gets in the way of the best plans and after 16 years of training I had to choose between more Kung Fu and passing my college courses. Don't think for a second I *wanted* to quit. Kenneth felt all along I made the wrong choice. For weeks he bemoaned the fact we were not going to the studio and attacked me from around corners and under blankets. His cry of "yak" preceded a swift strike & after three years drove me back to the studio out of self-preservation.

Chapter 15
Hospital Timeshare

Little boys get hurt. The sooner moms learn this fact the calmer everyone will be. The male hormone testosterone causes boys to act more impulsively, aggressively, and foolishly. In fact, guys who act that way probably have an overabundance of the big "T" along with deep voices, body hair and endless scars. Kenneth shall be their King.

We've decided to buy vacation space in the local emergency room. He has us there twice a week anyway; we might as well enjoy the stay.

***

Pencil Lip

Remember when your mom used to yell, "Don't jump on the bed! You'll fall off and..."? Mine did too. I used to trampoline from one bed to the other, bouncing off the walls in the process, and I NEVER got hurt. Of course, dad replaced our normal mattresses with water beds which made it much more of an adventure. It was like trying to launch from a bowl of jell-o.

Well, despite his parent's best verbal blasts, Kenneth loved to jump on our bed. He's already whacked his head into the ceiling fan twice and fell more often than I can count. These minor incidents made no difference to him at all. Seems he had to spill some blood before bed-jumping lost a bit of its fun.

This story begins (like so many others) with Kiff in the other room. I swear we watch the boy but do we *really* need to hover over him every second? My folks didn't and look how well I turned out. Forget that.

So Kiff is in the back of the house when we hear a soul-rending scream mixed with a booming crash. Heather and I fly down the hall and into our room where we find Kiff lying on the floor; half of 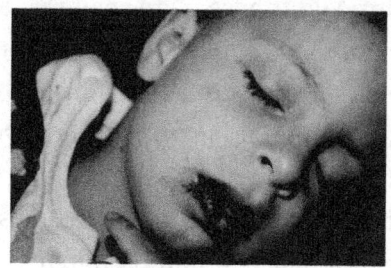 Heather's nightstand pulled over on top of him; and pools of blood all around.

Bless her heart, Heather was great. She took him in her arms and pulled his hands away so I could examine the lump of raw hamburger that was his lower lip. We knew fairly quickly that he was somewhere between needing stitches and bleeding-out so we lost no time in dialing 911.

We covered his face in a bath towel (no, not to smother him you evil people) and kept pressure on the cut. Then we raced across town to the hospital. By the time we got there I had a pretty good idea what happened.

I knew he was on the bed because the covers were mussed. It didn't take a Sherlock Holmes to guess he had been jumping. From there it was a natural progression to him toppling over onto mom's night stand where his face landed onto the cup of sharpened pencils she always kept there. He would of course roll off onto the floor and drag the pencils, cup, books, magazines and chocolate with him. All of these were scattered about the floor and one pencil in particular was covered in deep red ooze.

The doctors and nurses were very good and stitched him up in a jiffy. He never seemed to be in much pain after the first injury and the scar is minimal except when he laughs. Then it becomes a bold white patch. I think it makes him look tough.

***

All I Want for Christmas…

Heather told me this one because I wasn't home when it happened:

Kenneth does learn from his mistakes. He just doesn't get the lesson *we* would have expected. He stopped jumping on the bed so much because it's dangerous. So he began climbing on the dining room table.

Like many families, we have the large oak set with leaves to seat 35. Its weight is somewhere upwards of a bull elephant and sturdy enough to build a small apartment building on if necessary. Kiff must have felt

116

perfectly safe while dancing up there, until gravity had its way with him once again. Actually I cannot blame the Law this time because the little brainiac decided he was going to jump off.

Heather didn't see it happen but then here comes Kenneth walking up to his mommy, hands covering his 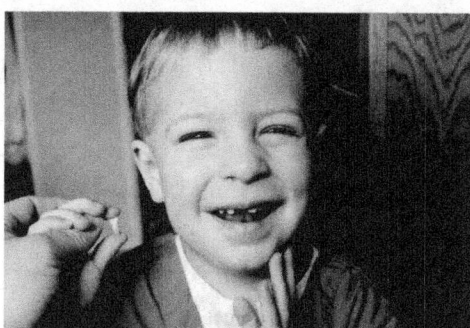 face and blood dripping all over the carpet. I think she may have screamed this time but she won't admit it.

She checked him over and was relieved and confused to find nothing wrong. Where had all the blood come from? Not until she examined him three times did she notice that his right front tooth was missing. Not chipped or broken mind you. It was completely gone!

He proudly told her all about how he was a superhero and had flown off the table but the "bad guys" made him crash into the ground. If by "bad guys" he means the combined forces of physics and an early "Darwin Award" application, well then he would be right.

Not too many days later we decided to take down the table for his own good. Not that it helped much.

***

117

The boy doesn't always suffer physical injuries. Sometimes he just gets sick. Like the time we went to The Sizzler. The place isn't bad and certainly not nauseating. Of course, Kiff would disagree.

Not 10 minutes after we began to eat Kenneth whispered, "Daddy, I don't feel good." Then he promptly vomited all over the table. He flooded his own plate with the first wave and doused mine with the second. By then Heather had snatched her own food and whisked it into the neighboring booth.

I don't want to be overly graphic but it was projectile vomiting. He got everything. The staff came out with towels and had to bring on the mop and bucket to get control of the rising tide. His third bout soaked the floor all around us and the fourth left a slimy trail right through the dining room as Heather tried to get him into the lavatory.

They had a devil of a time cleaning up. I suspect the fire they had months later was a last ditch effort to sterilize the place or just collect the insurance money. We haven't been back to that location since.

***

118

When he gets sick, he gives it his all and falls asleep right there.

***

On rare occasion, Heather and I are able to intercept young Dexter and prevent some tragedy or another.

The Hidden Lab

Kenneth walked past us one evening and disappeared into the garage. Heather and I were engrossed in *Whose Line is it Anyway?* and thought nothing of it. Soon he walked out carrying the wooden ladder which had hung on his bunk bed for years. It was taken away due to Kiff's irritating habit of climbing on top of any flat surface he could find.

As he passed by I asked, "Kenneth, where are you going with that ladder?" Without blinking an eye he said, "To my room." I don't know why the answer didn't faze me. Maybe I was just so shocked by his truthfulness that it didn't sink in for several seconds.

We stared at his retreating bottom and then each other before coming to our senses. Quietly, we tip-toed down the hall and then leaned around the corner; just peeking into his room. The first thing I saw was the large, heavy oak tabletop. It was wedged against a dresser and the spare entertainment center. The second thing I noticed was Kenneth standing, quite proudly I must say,

119

atop the dresser. Since he had disposed of the window curtains some time ago this was now his own private stage. I am sure the neighbors were sitting on their porches, eating popcorn and preparing to call Child Protective Services, but I digress.

We walked in and asked him what exactly he was doing.

"I'm making a lab", he answered deliberately.

There before us was a triangular space about three foot to a side and five feet deep, created behind the tabletop (did I mention that it is large and very heavy)? Inside rested a collection of tinker toys which Kiff had rescued from Gunny Bag earlier in the week. Standing against the dresser, inside this "lab" was the ladder he had purloined just minutes earlier. I can only surmise that he used the ladder to climb onto the dresser; summoned the help of a few dozen evil demons to grant him the strength to not only tilt but reposition the 50 pound table (did I mention it is solid oak); then lifted up the ladder and dropped it into his secret lab.

Just as any good parents would do when faced with a potentially dangerous situation involving their child Heather asked, "Have you been in your lab yet?" Whereupon he descended the ladder and we pulled it up, trapping him in the snare of his own creation.

He howled terribly as we laughed and told him that youth and imagination will always lose to age and treachery. I do take solace in the fact he offered a very heartfelt "thanks" when we gave him back the ladder. At least out little serial killer will have manners.

***

Other Times He Catches Us Off-Guard

One advantage of living somewhere which used to be a Primordial Sea is being able to go excavating for fossils. Within 10 miles of our home sits Shark's Tooth Mountain wherein lie thousands of Shark's Teeth. We're not a very creative bunch here. In addition to the teeth are bits of skeleton and other detritus from ancient sea life. Though easiest to find at STM, any of the hills off to the east are likely to give-up a treasure or two if one is willing to get a little dirty.

And now, the Kiff story: Two of Heather's sisters came to visit. Since they are  not your namby-pamby girly-girls, they all wanted to go looking for teeth. After climbing a tall and steep hill, everyone settled down to gouge out the compressed sand and dirt wall.

Kenneth, who usually loves any form of destruction, quickly grew bored and began doing what any normal boy that age would do. Naturally, everyone got dirt in their eyes and we were lucky no one had to go to the emergency room for corneal scratches.

***

Bakersfield can get hot in the summer. Right now we are enjoying a long stretch of 105 degree days followed by 85 degree nights. As a result everyone is grouchy, touchy and dehydrated. I'm drinking a gallon of water a day and am still thirsty. One effect of all this pre-death mummification is that various membranes get hard and crack with the slightest touch. Not good for little nose-pickers with busy fingers.

Late in the evening I ordered Kiff to get ready for bed. From out of the nightmarish depths of his bedroom I hear a panicked voice cry, "Mahhhhhh-meeeee, my nose is bleeding."

Heather was in the shower so I calmly took the boy in hand and led him to the bathroom sink.

"Just let it bleed son. We'll wash it off and rinse out the gunk. It'll stop soon."

Now stop yelling at me. I know you are supposed to tilt the head back and pinch off the bridge of the nose until it sets. But I wanted him to learn not to be afraid of blood, particularly his own.

So we stood there for a few seconds, a quick flow of red dribbling down his face and into the basin. I spoke

122

in a soothing voice and assured him that everything would be fine. Finally I got to the point.

"Kenneth, why is your nose bleeding?"

"I don't know." Have we gotten to *that* stage already?

"Kenneth, were you picking your nose?"

"We-ll, my nose picking laser was picking my nose and I think it cut my brain."

Later Heather asked him again and he showed how the laser went way far up into the nose and worked both sides for good measure.

That's my boy.

***

You would think at some point the kid would begin to learn from his various injuries. Maybe slow down a bit or even think before he acted. No such luck.

Monday evening I walked down the hall and noticed Kiff in a most unusual position: floating five feet in the air. I rubbed my eyes and looked again. Oh, everything was fine, he's only four feet up. What?!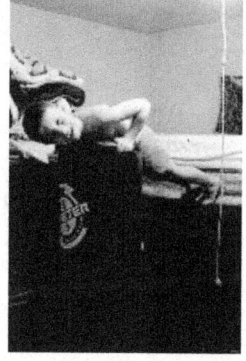

He glanced up into my concerned face and said, "Oh, hi Daddy. I am doing air push-ups. Wanna see?" At which point he proceeded to do six perfectly executed push-ups in mid air!

Granted, the room was dark and I was half-asleep. It took me a minute to register that his toes were hooked into the frame of the top bunk bed while his body spanned out into the wild blue wonder. His arms were solidly atop my free-standing punching bag!

Being the careful and loving father that I am, I grabbed the camera and took a few snaps to prove I wasn't seeing things.

***

And so we go on and on with little Kenneth having no fear in the world and the Eddy's single-handedly propping-up the American Health Care System.

Chapter 16
Mingos and Sharp Parts

This chapter holds the honor of bearing the book's title not because it is especially funny or even that long. It is however one of the earliest examples of Kenneth being absolutely bizarre.

***

I don't have the slightest idea where this meme came from. At about three he suddenly began traipsing through the house yammering about Mingos and Sharp Parts. I, like Snape, put my keen and penetrating mind to the task and came up with the wrong conclusion. Because I assumed he had finally discovered that some things can cut you and that wasn't very fun darn it. How very wrong I was.

The boys were playing with a deck of cards and Alex asked Kiff if he knew the names of the suits. One by one AJ showed him a card and Kenneth tried to guess.

"Red heart"

"Red diamond"

"Red diamond"

"Black mingo"

"What?" I said. "What did you call that?"

"That's a mingo", answered Kenneth.

"No buddy. That's a club."

He shook his tiny head as if to say it was a shame I had become senile so soon and went on with his game.

"Red heart"

"Black sharp part"

"Sharps parts? Alex, is that a spade?"

"Yea dad."

"Kenneth Calvin…these", I said holding up a card, "are clubs." I held another, "and these are spades."

No amount of arguing could bring him around to my obviously flawed way of thinking.

But the mystery doesn't end there. The next day Mack told me that clubs are called mingos because they look like the footprints of a flamingo. And of course spades are sometimes associated with spearheads and so they would indeed be 'sharp parts'.

Well, there ya go: puzzle solved. That is until Kiff began to educate me in the birds and the bees. Because according to him mingos are girls and sharp parts are boys. Think about it. Then I ask myself, "Who's been showing him pictures of human anatomy?"

Chapter 17
Suffer the Little Children?

The Eddy's go to church. Oh boy do we go.
Heather and I are very religious people and proudly
belong to The Church of Jesus Christ of Latter-Day Saints
or Mormons as we are often called. Yes there are some
fundamental differences between our form of Christianity
and the others, just as there are profound differences
between Catholics and Evangelicals; Baptists and 7th-Day
Adventists; Russian Orthodox and the Church of England.
However, there are also some basic similarities.

For this story you need to understand that every
Sunday we have a rite or ceremony called The Sacrament.
It has roughly the same purpose and symbolism as
Communion. Unlike Catholic parishioners who rise and
go to the priest to receive the wafer, we pass around little
trays hand-to-hand which hold bread torn into bite-sized
pieces.

A Deacon held the try for Heather and she partook
of the bread. She then held it for Kenneth. For a second I
thought he'd gone blind because he touched each and
every piece of bread in the tray. Bad enough he played
with everyone else's Holy Sacrament, I heard a quiet
chuckle from the people behind us.

"No Kiff!" I hissed. "Don't touch them all. Just
take one."

"I'm looking for one without crust", he said in a moderate voice. Then loud as a bull horn, "Why does everyone make me eat the crust?"

I wonder if the Church will ever open a monastery.

***

Once the sermons were underway Kiff got bored. Frankly I did too but… He suddenly raised his fists into Heather's face and began trying to box with her.

"Kenneth, what are you doing? Stop it!" she whispered.

"The bread told me to fight."

Her shock was beyond words.

Exasperated by his mother's complete inability to understand such a simple idea, he sighed and explained, "On the two green days I fight, but not on the red days. Today is a red day."

So I guess he wasn't fighting until the bread told him to. It must have been sourdough.

***

Yesterday was full of memorable Kiffisms.

During The Sacrament I corrected him on how it is performed.

"Daddy, why do we use the right hand and not the left?"

"Well, we use the right hand in making a promise. We raise it when taking an oath. We place it on the Bible

128

when swearing to tell the truth in court. We even use it when we shake hands. It is symbolic. The Sacrament is all about promising to follow Jesus and be His disciple, so we use the right hand."

He thought deeply about this for a few seconds and then his face brightened into a joyful grin.

"When we play church later we can use either hand."

I see a Great Schism coming our way.

***

Kiff listened carefully to the bread because he just would not stop squirming. And his volume dial kept edging upwards. I tried all the normal parental techniques. I gave him The Look. I tapped him on the shoulder and then the head. Finally I placed him on my lap and whispered that he would stay here for a while if he couldn't behave.

The next moment he began to sing loudly. I cupped my hand over his mouth and whispered in his ear something about selling him to the gypsies. Evidently he was prepared for this move because he started to lick my fingers and then blew his nose all over my hand.

Eww!

I had no handkerchief or tissues, so I wiped off the gooey sticky mess onto the inside of his shirttails.

What would you do?

***

The child did not seem to think much of my snotty solution. He quieted down for a while…biding his time. After about 15 minutes he grew loud again and I (not having learned the first time), once more covered his mouth. His response was forceful and effective.

 Hard to believe that such a tiny jaw could produce so many pounds of force. His teeth sank deep into my finger. But in this battle of wills, I was not going to let him win. Not for naught had I been a youngest child and more than once my brothers tried to use pain to intimidate me. I refused to give the child satisfaction.

The ridiculousness of this situation is hard to describe. Here I am in my best suit, my wife looking stunningly pretty at my side in a house of worship, and my finger clamped tightly in the maul of a rabid pit-bull named Kenneth.

Tears may have formed. I hardly remember through the haze of agony. But still I did not give in to his sadistic demands. Eventually he relented and opened his mouth to reveal my mangled digit feebly trying to move.

As if wishing to memorialize the epic battle, he fell to his crayons with a will.

It looks like he may need to visit the dentist.

***

Once Kiff gets to drawing he's quite prolific. He will produce five, six, seven or more pictures in quick succession. Here are a couple of the ones he made along with the "Finger Bite":

The Evil Rain-

A bright red E marks the evil rain as it tries to overcome the three bright suns, vertical blue rain and horizontal blue wind. I don't get it either.

 Battle for Freedom-

Christ is holding a blue flag marked Freedom as He goes into battle with Satan whose flag reads "Evil". Kiff's cousin Donovan (who died seven years before Kenneth's own birth) is there as a spirit to cheer on the Savior.

***

Most churches have some sort of children's program or ministry. Let's face it; you have to start teaching them young nowadays to compete with lewd cartoons and social media. Ours is called Primary and Kenneth loves it.

In particular he likes his teacher Sister Judy, though that was not always the case. She is a tall, kind and rather pretty brunette. She and her husband just moved into our Ward and we did not know her well.

131

Imagine my shock and embarrassment when she brought Kenneth at the end of church and informed me that he told her she was ugly.

I'm beginning to think the kid might be blind after all.

We talked at home.

"Kenneth, why did you say Sister Judy was ugly?"

"Because she made me stop doing what I wanted to do."

"That does not make her ugly. That makes her a good teacher."

"Well I think she is ugly inside because she made me stop."

While I think he's wrong, the logic is rather sound.

***

As devout Christians we hold the Sabbath to be a holy day and try to keep it sacred. This means avoiding normal pursuits in favor of worship, service to others, family time and personal religious study. I must confess that I do watch the Super Bowl every year but as it is spent with my father it is more in the realm of strengthening our relationship…or so I tell Heather.

As a result of this devotion I am continually telling the boys that "we do not play sports on Sunday". For the most part this is extended to video games as well though educational games are winked at.

Why am I telling you all this? Because Kenneth just made a proclamation to his mother which, if true, would cause a wholesale reordering of Christianity.

"I want to go play hockey with my friends."

"No Kenneth, we don't play sports on Sunday."

"But I'm the one who made Sunday. And when I made Sunday I said that you *could* play sports on Sunday."

"Oh really?"

"Yea, but then the person who made this earth re-phrased it and made it just backwards and it made me SO ANGRY!!"

Um…do I see lightning clouds gathering?

***

We, of course, are teaching Kenneth to say his prayers. Unlike some traditions which have set prayers to be said exactly according to pattern, we simply talk to our Father in Heaven, asking Him for what we need and thanking Him for blessings given.

This evening we encouraged Kiff to add a bit more variety to the prayer he has been saying. His new requests were for "cool uniforms to fight a little bit of evil" and to have "more strength than was possible".

***

My mother died this past spring after several years of illness. Kenneth will sometimes talk to her. She is still a very real person even though she has gone to the 'other side'.

He just handed Heather a picture of Mom, complete with wings, halo and glasses.

"Kiff, why is she wearing glasses?"

"Cause she's watching me...*al-ways watching*."

Think Roz from Monsters Inc.

***

At three years old the little ones move from the nursery into what we call Primary. This is the Sunday School program for kids up to 12 when they move into Young Men's and Young Women's.

It seems that Kenneth was not interested in the lesson as planned by the teachers. At least he raised his hand before speaking.

"Sister Villanueva, I don't think we should sing that song."

"Kenneth, we are singing these songs right now."

"But I don't think we should sing them."

"Okay, what song do you think we *should* sing?"

"Did you know *I like honey*?"

***

His contrarianism went well beyond the music. He also seems to have a problem with scripture. Sister V. called us this evening to share an amusing story.

They were reading in the Old Testament when Kenneth raised his hand.

134

"I'm going to destroy the Reign of the Judges with my super powers."

What is he Sampson now?

Chapter 18
My Bottom Said a Bad Word

I believe this little gem will set the tone for the whole chapter:

Kenneth walked into the living room after a nice long bath; his hair and limbs still dripping profusely because he completely forgot to towel off. He looked Heather deep in the eyes and said in a most repentant tone, "Mommy, my bottom said a bad word."

"What did your bottom say?" she asked.

"I can't tell you."

"Whisper it in my ear."

Whereupon he spoke a certain very crude word for a very beautiful act of love and companionship. After she got over the shock of hearing her dear little boy say such a thing she told him, "I don't want your bottom to say that ever again or it will get a spanking."

"Okay Mommy. My bottom won't say it anymore." Then he smiled innocently.

While Heather is a bright and insightful woman, she just may have been suckered by this one. "My *bottom* won't say it anymore", indeed.

***

One bright and glorious Sunday afternoon, Heather, Kenneth and I drove up into the mountains which surround Bakersfield. Nestled in the high vales out

136

toward the eastern desert is a town christened Tehachapi. Heather was extended an invitation by their arts community to display some of her folded books in an art show and we decided to make a family outing of her need to deliver the *objects d'arte.*

Some hours earlier Heather gave a talk in church about the Temple and how it affected her life. As we drove, Heather leaned toward me and whispered, "At least I didn't say *those* two words."

You need to remember that Heather and I are…earthy type people. Occasionally we might tell a slightly bawdy or even ribald joke. Just between us you know.

Immediately Kenneth asked, "Mooooooom, what happens if I say those two words?"

"What two words babe?"

"*Those* two words!"

Unable to let unspoken profanity lie…unspoken, Heather persisted. "You tell me which two words you mean."

Little prepared was I for the cannonade which shot from the back seat, "BOOBS AND HOES!"

After she managed to get the car back into our lane, Heather and I smiled warmly to each other; both of us thinking, "Your genes."

***

The following story is not strictly about bad words but… (hee hee I said butt again). Heather just walked into my office and shared her conversation with Kiff.

He explained to her that testicles make seeds: pink seeds and blue seeds and he very much wanted to know which ones made which color.

"Who told you about that?" she queried.

"You did."

"Really, why would I tell that to a 5 year old?"

His answer was a giggle.

"I don't have those", Heather told the grinning child.

"Why not?"

"Because I'm not lucky."

"Why aren't you lucky?"

She muttered something in reply about not having to do house work or being sensitive to others. I don't know, I wasn't listening.

***

Occasionally our congregation at church will have visitors. I don't mean the usual people interested in hearing what our religion may have to say or family in for the week-end. I refer to Church Leadership. Where Catholics have Priests and Baptists have Pastors, we have Bishops. The next level above the Priest is the Catholic Bishop who presides over a number of diocese. Our

138

equivalent is the Stake President. He watches over 8-12 Wards (congregations) with their Bishops.

One day our Stake President came to visit. I happen to know him personally since he was in a Scout Troop led by my mother decades before and our families socialized from time to time.

Once again we attended Sacrament Meeting. Our Bishop, his counselors, the Stake President, one of his counselors, and numerous other visitors were all listening intently to the speaker. The only one in the room not doing so was our very own Kenneth Calvin George Eddy.

The boy grew progressively louder with his toys and I urged him most sincerely to remain reverent. He did not think this was a very good idea. Finally I looked him straight in the face and said, rather fiercely, "Kenneth, you need to stop talking right now!"

With eyes full of protest at this unwarranted attack he proclaimed to the entire assembly that, "I *didn't* say the f-word!!"

Wow. Just wow.

***

Another story that, while not about bad words, is still amusing word play.

On my way to the bathroom I said hi to Kiff through his doorway. He immediately called back that I was, "The Wicked Witch of the West".

"No, I'm a boy. I would have to be the Wicked Warlock of the West."

And shut the door in his face.

His voice rang down the hall, "You are the Wicked Witch of the…"

But I cut him off.

"Maybe I'm the Nasty Necromancer of the North. Or maybe the Silly Sorcerer of the South. Oh, how about the Evil Enchanter of the East?"

"You are the Wicked Warlock of the West Room."

I groan at the pun, whether he meant it or not.

***

No person with a grasp of reality can dispute that our language has become coarser over the last few decades. What would once have landed a person in jail for 'blue' talk is now used in the title of TV shows. The whole mess just makes me sad.

One result is an increase of foul language in video games. Because little Kenneth must go to the sitter every day, and because we cannot ban *them* from playing whatever games they wish, it is an unfortunate result that Kiff's vocabulary has become much more colorful.

Just the other day he and Heather were playing *Bubble Safari* on Facebook when Kiff began to encourage his mother.

"Let's kick some crazy a** bubbles!"

We told him his bubbles would be popped if they didn't clean-up their act.

***

I supposed the child has called my bluff, and using 'plausible deniability' too. On Thursdays the kids and I stop at my father's for a couple hours of socializing while Heather is still at work. They miss their Grandmother and I want them to know my dad while they can.

The older ones, my sister, Dad and I were playing cards while Kenneth spent quality time with a can of crayons and ream of paper. Whenever he finished a picture he would shove it into the face of whomever it was created for. All except one which I saw him carefully tuck under the others.

I became a little suspicious and so asked him to show me the drawing.

"Okay daddy, but I can't spell all the words."

"What words?"

He just smiled and tried to look demure. I will let you decide what he meant to say.

Chapter 19
I am Your Tiny Husband

I want to marry a gal just like the gal that married dear old dad.

It's natural for boys to see their mom as the perfection of womanhood. She is their most prominent feminine role model and any sisters will likely reflect mom anyway. Kenneth, like countless lads before him, has decided he is going to marry his mother. Deep and profound is Kiff's love for Heather. He brings her presents and gives *her* all the hugs and kisses. Frankly, the boy is far more romantic than I've ever been.

Last night he actually left off playing Angry Birds in order to draw his mommy a picture. It is a study of the things he loves the most:

Looking at this modern masterpiece with a critical eye, one first notices the bright bold use of a red marker. The powerful, almost maniacal strokes show the artist's passion about his subject. Heading the portrait with the word LOVE declares to the whole universe that "this is more than just infatuation".

142

Almost sub-consciously he shows by the upside-down house that he wants to upend the current status quo. Perhaps this has something to do with chapter 21?

As we continue in a counter-clockwise direction, the simple heart, again containing love, demarks the beginning of what he longs for. He loves his mother's legs for he can cling to them when he's afraid. He loves her torso for it is warm and cuddly; with arms to hold him tight. He loves her hands for all the candy they give and her neck because it is ticklish. He loves her (bald) head because she smiles at him. And of course, he loves pizza. One must NEVER forget the pizza.

***

What woman could resist the charms of such a funny, sweet and devoted suitor? He dotes on her every word and swoons whenever she bestows a kiss on his cheek. Before long Kenneth decided it was time to bring his true feelings to her attention.

"Mommy, I want to marry you."

"I'm sorry Kenneth, you can't marry me. I am already married to Daddy and that would be polygamy which is in fact frowned upon in the United States." (Forgive her Mr. Wonka)

"Well, I will kill him and then you can marry me."

"Kiff, you are not going to kill your daddy."

A look of murderous disdain flashed across his face as he turned toward me.

"Besides, you are too young to get married."

He thought for a moment, brightened considerably and then said, "I can be your tiny husband!"

Is there a law against *pediogamy*?

***

As with many husbands he developed an aversion to clothes. After one bath he walked into the living room wrapped in a towel but not held closed, bravely waggling his personality for all to see. I asked him to go get dressed.

"Oh no! Not again."

He went to his room and then a few minutes later came out, pushing some cars, heine up in the air like a stink bug. The instant he saw me he stood up, ran back to his room, butt cheeks covered by both hands, screaming.

***

Kenneth is well on his way to becoming a husband for he loves to sit in his underwear and ogle the TV. Not in the way a sports fan craves the game or some women are addicted to soaps. Kenneth worships at the altar of big Hollywood movies. Occasionally we feel the need to keep the boob tube off for the evening (I know, call Child Protective Services). Just a few minutes ago Heather had to punish him. Asking for the TV about 15 times in 1 minute AFTER being told no is generally not the best plan. Later I walked into his room and found him cross-legged on the floor, surround by the great mass of his toys and determinedly working on a "project".

Me: What are you building son?

Kiff: A machine to stop Mom from ever doing anything bad to me again.

Me: And you think that will really work?

Kiff: Uh-huh, because it's a *Stop Everything From Hurting Me* machine. My machine hot powers from my room, into the hallway, and into the art room and up to her chair. And it does lots of stuff. It keeps flipping the power into her chair but when she eats a cookie her face will have no more goose bumps after she eats one bite of one cookie. I hooked the cookies to her chair and I didn't make the machine yet so that's why I borrowed some pieces from her in case I don't make it to the art room.

145

And the machine gloops after I make the machine and then it blows the power out and goes into my mother's chair and into the cookies and then the Goosebumps will be gone.

I'm not sure he understands the purpose and function of a revenge machine. For the most part, making goose bumps go away is a good thing.

***

Hard as it is to believe, there once was a time when little children knew nothing about intimacy. They simply did not understand what adults did behind closed doors. Today they openly discuss the topic of sex apparently without shame.

Kenneth is somewhere in between. He's painfully aware that we are doing something and having a lot of fun at it. Every time Heather and I closed the door he is sure to come barging in within a few minutes.

Some months back, after he managed to kick open the door and share our special moment, I installed small bolt locks at the top and bottom of the door. His fury was something to behold the first time he could not come in as he pleased. Heh heh heh.

Now whenever the door is barred against him he will stand outside and talk to us.

"Mommy, is it okay if your diet Pepsi accidentally falls into a cup?"

"No!" I cry out. "It must stay in the bottle!"

"Mommy, let me in so I can fire your husband."

He waited until I left the room a while later. He had a wooden pole set inside a foam tube which I use for kung fu training. They may be safer but pack quite a sting.

I ran out the door and hid in the bathroom before he could get a good shot.

***

Have you ever seen the old movie *Gaslight*? Well I think Kenneth and Heather are trying to convince me I am insane.

I called home this morning, just to say I loved them and hoped they would have a good day. The phone was answered by (I could have sworn) a frail little old lady. "Must have dialed the wrong number", I thought. Then the weirdness started.

"H-h-h-e-llllloooo?" came the voice.

"I'm sorry. I dialed the wrong number."

"I-i-is this someone I should know?"

"No ma'am. I'm sorry. Have a nice…"

"You sure sound funny on the speaker phone."

"Kenneth, is that you? Why did you answer the phone? Let me talk to your mother."

In the meantime I hear maniacal laughter erupt in the background.

It's all fun and games until someone gets checked into the asylum.

***

As with most marriages, Heather and Kiff have their ups and downs. Sometimes Kenneth is a bit more aggressive with Heather. This evening he did not want to go take a bath. She told him he must do so to which he responded that he was Super Kenneth and did not have to. Heather reminded him she was still in charge and he would do as she said. His answer was classic, "That is because you are a Clock American but that does not lessen my superness."

148

We enjoy lazy Saturday afternoons at home, listening to music and sorting through our various collected books. Heather was kneeling on the floor examining a very old children's primer when Kiff suddenly leapt upon her back, wrapped his arms around her neck and cooed, "We are in love."

She was a bit taken aback and said sternly, "No Kenneth. I love you but I am in love with Daddy."

None but an accomplished actor or one deeply infatuated with his true soul mate could purr out words as smoothly as Kiff did. "I am in love with you. And you are in love with me. And we are in love together."

I sat on the couch, watching my marriage dissolve, another man usurping my place in her heart.

***

Heather was almost in tears when she told me this story:

I was asleep in bed when something began poking me in the back. I tried to move away but it just kept on poking. Finally I rolled over and opened my eyes to find Kenneth right in my face staring at me.

"Mommy, I love you", he purred and then began making fish lips at me.

I would have paid to see that one.

***

Sometimes I am just a passive observer to his antics. Last night Heather and I prepared for bed when she suddenly perked up like a foxhound catching the scent. Her head slowly turned toward the door and then screamed, "Kiff, stop doing that!"

I had no idea what was going on but some random sound just on the horizon of my hearing continued.

"Kenneth! Stop it now!"

Into the room slinks our kind sweet little boy who asks, "Mommy, how do you know what I am doing when you can't see me?"

In typical parent-speak she replied, "I'm the Momma. I know things."

"Well, you know things in your brain that aren't really there."

I'd have gone to the woodshed for saying something like that to *my* momma.

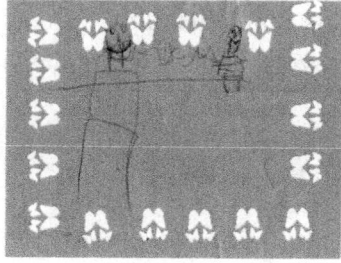 Kenneth loves to use Heather's scrap booking tools. He'll find the hole-punch and just tear into a piece of paper. Sometimes he will run the edges and write something in the middle. I put before you a certain creation. Please note the little boy who looks suspiciously like my son, shooting his laser at the momma to "make her zip her lip" any time she tells him something he doesn't like.

***

Sadly, like many relationships, Kiff and Heather's future life together appears doubtful. She is taking it stoically though. I will allow heather to tell the story from her Facebook page:

Kiff just ate a ring pop. He says to me, "I'm going to keep this ring. That way women will want to marry me and men will want to BE me."

Where did he get that?

***

My dear wife and her darling son just came home from lunch at the Golden Arches. He was deliriously happy and she was out of sorts. Immediately Heather started vacuuming the floors while shoved his fingers in his ears.

"Daddy, why are vacuums so loud?"

"That is the sound of the air going into the vacuum and taking the dirt with it."

"When I get older and have power tools, I will invent a vacuum that doesn't make any noise at all. That way it won't hurt my ears."

Heather popped her head into the room and asked, "Kenneth, who's going to do the vacuuming in your house once you get married?"

"My new wife will do the vacuuming…like she should."

Why do I feel the need to apologize? I've never said anything like that. In front of him. Since I was a stupid teenager.

Chapter 20
Clock America

Most parents are amused when their child creates a fantasy world in which to play. Indeed, a kid who didn't retreat into the mental ether occasionally would be cause for concern. Healthy imaginations promote objective thinking, outside-the-box solutions and make one far more interesting at every stage of life.

Kenneth, on the other hand, displays a knack for creativity that would make Disney-on-PCP say, "Where the heck did *that* come from?" For your consideration, I present the mighty Empire of Clock America.

***

My first visit to this magical land came one afternoon after retrieving Kenneth from his aunt's.

"Daddy, where are we going?"

"We're going home son. I have some things to do."

"We can't go home. We have to go to Clock America."

He was only 4 years old; easily influenced; and fresh from spending all day with his female cousins, strange ideas were not unexpected. Maybe I simply misheard. So I prompted him a little.

"Did you mean *South* America?" I queried.

"Nnnnnnooooooo, Clock America!" The sarcasm fairly burned with disdain. "It's a place far away in the north over by Germany."

"Oh really? You don't mean France or Belgium do you?"

"Daddy, Clock America is between Germany and the ocean to the north."

I stifled the sarcasm and retorted, "Kiff, there isn't much between Germany and the North Sea. Some, sandy beaches is about all."

"Yes, that's where it is. It's a city on the beach of Germany and they like to be called Clock America. And they are very fierce. And they don't like you."

For once I was speechless (and those who have known me for a while realize how utterly improbable THAT condition is). "They don't like me?"

"No, because you are an anti-Clock American."

***

Unlike most of Kiff's brainstorms which last only a few days, Clock America is enduring. The story has grown in scope and detail until now I almost believe in it myself. Shame prevents me from telling the details but I've actually had dreams about the place.

Once Kiff gets an idea into his head, it is the central focus of his existence. Simply *everything* in our lives had some connection to Clock America and each person he met was soon judged as either a friend or foe of his homeland. Most of the family was okay because he brought them along when he came here. I, however, was most certainly <u>not</u> a Clock American.

Still, it is my humble duty and honor to act as scribe for Kenneth in telling the world about this land of beauty and joy.

***

THE store in Clock America (for of course there is only one…duh) sells shirts. They have one aisle for white shirts and one aisle for colored shirts. Across from the shirt aisle is the toy aisle.

Mom: How much do the toys cost?

Kiff: $200

155

Mom: And where do you get so much money?

Kiff: I just hold out my hand and it falls into my hand from out of the air.

Obviously my son is a Democrat.

**

It took a month of continual Clock America trivia before I finally learned to avoid the subject. After all, there was healthy imagination and then there was obsession. But his joy in the distant land of his birth never seemed to abate.

"I must tell you one thing", he said with a steely look in his eye, "just one thing. All the buildings in Clock America have burnt down except one."

"Really, just one building left?"

"Well, um", (um happens to be his absolute favorite word; I have omitted all but the most pertinent ones in order to keep my "u" and "m" keys from wearing out). "There's more than one building that didn't burn down. Maybe *3 million* buildings didn't burn down."

"Oh, that's a lot of buildings."

"Yea but *you* can't touch anything except one thing."

"And what is it that I *can* touch?"

"Well, you can touch the buttons that make you go up and down in the elevator in my house."

"Oh that's nice but I can't touch anything else?"

"Well, I have a bathroom in my house and a shower and a toi-let and you can touch those."

Poor kid, growing up in Bakersfield there are certain two syllable words that are pronounced with an unaccented pause in between. Say toilet in your head with a short "uh" between the toi and the let.

At least I need not bring a porta-potty when I finally visit Clock America.

***

Kenneth is very interested in this book. He seemed to think it a wonderful idea and the whole world would like to read about him. I really should say "all the worlds" because of course, Clock America *is* another world.

As I shared the first few paragraphs of chapter one with Heather, he forced his way onto my lap; asked what I was writing; and proceeded to tell me that he was, "...from another pla-eh-net called Clock America"

This was the first time I learned his fantasy land was *not* a large and precariously situated German city after all.

I was really shocked. Kenneth informed me he was not only knowledgeable of Clock America, he was from there. This explained so much. His mother and I breathed a sigh of relief that our very abnormal earth kid was a not-so-odd alien instead. Of course, that does bring up some rather awkward questions...

***

Clock America is apparently part of the Star Wars Universe. Kiff told me one day about a huge meeting held so that the people could sort out their lightsabers. They have red, yellow, green, purple and blue. Later I discovered the people in that galaxy know it as Mustafar from *SW:III Revenge of the Sith*.

***

The people of Clock America love

contests, all kinds. The boy walked into my room and showed me a handful of expired glow sticks (there is *almost* enough material for a whole chapter just on that toy). He proudly proclaimed that, "This is my glow stick collection to win the Glow Stick Collection Competition of Clock America. You wanna know what the trophy is made of?"

"Glow sticks?" I asked sarcastically.

"Yeh-sssssssssssss", he enthused.

***

Clock American's like music, especially choir music. Not surprisingly, Kiff was a choir director back home. He told me about an incident once.

"I love you Kiff."

He scrambled over and gave me a huge embrace, then seemed to think better of such a public display of affection.

"Well, you get *one* hug."

"But I love you."

He looked very thoughtful, almost meditative.

"I will make a golden statue out of paper and a golden egg and this is about the choir I taught on Clock America and I played the piano."

"Uhhh."

"And you taught them bad stuff but I came in and untaught them and then I turned it tricky."

O-kay.

***

The choir theme has continued for the last few days. Late this evening he very seriously told me about the solemn origins of his group.

"Dad, I want to tell you about that tricky choir practice. In 1984, which was long before I was born, the President of Clock America said, 'Let's build a choir practice indoors and make it not of singing."

He then let out a long and soul-cleansing sigh. One would think he had just confessed to the Simpson Murders.

"Oh, and make sure you write that down!"

He wants to read about himself, once he learns to read.

He just informed me that he was born that very auspicious day and that is how he knew about the pronouncement.

***

Strange how so many of these stories begin with "I walk into the bedroom…" Perhaps I should put a child-proof latch on my door.

SO, I walk into the bedroom and Kiff is standing atop a barstool looking adventurous. I quickly ask what he thinks he is doing. As if I really *wanted* to know.

"I am showing my invisible friends about how when I taught a boys and girls choir on Clock America and I showed them an omni-trick."

"An omni-trick?"

"Yes, an omni-trick. I would ask if everyone had a barstool. When they answered yes I showed them how to jump from their favorite colored barstool onto their parent's bed like this…"

Perhaps the years of Kung Fu training sharpened my reactions; or maybe just a sixth sense for danger kicked in; all I know is as soon as he said the word 'jump' I reacted. His leap was spectacular, six feet from a

161

standing position. At least it would have had I not snatched him out of mid-air.

To this day he is angry I ruined his story.

**

As might be guessed, the technology on Clock America is far in advance of our own. None of these slow and mistake prone typing or video interfaces. They developed a far more efficient and handy way of using their computers.

Kenneth and I were coming home from a hockey game one evening. A friend who works for the team gave him an extra hockey stick set (shh, don't tell anyone). He began showering her with praise, how nice she was and all about how, when he was three, she had blown bubbles and let him jump and try to catch them. But he never got any. I didn't believe him and said of course he had gotten some.

"No", he insisted, "the computer in my tummy tells me that I never got any bubbles."

"How did you get a computer in your tummy"?

"In Clock America you can buy a mini-computer for one $100 bill."

"How did you get it in your tummy?" I asked.

"Well you put it in with a needle."

A little nervous about my son an sharp things I asked, "What have you done with your needle?"

"Well I had two needles because I bought two computers and put them in my tummy with the computers I got in Clock America. But I lost the needles on my way to this planet."

"How did you lose them?"

"Well I gave them to the computers in my tummy because I didn't need them anymore and they gave the needles to the son-computer which is the smaller computer in Clock America."

I hesitate to ask what the son-computer needs with all these needles.

***

With deep regret I must confess, Clock Americans have a few social ills in common with Earthlings. Remember back in chapter 18 when Kenneth asked about "those two words"? Well, he proceeded to inform us that on Clock America adults can say those words. They do not get embarrassed by saying them. They can "sing

163

them; and write them; and even use them in their prayers". I am a bit concerned about exactly which God the C.A.'s pray too if they ask about boobs and hoes often enough to make it memorable. Of course they might be flat-chested gardeners for all I know.

***

Kenneth is always trying to be helpful, especially with younger children. He will shush with the best of them whenever someone is too loud. Once he dragged a 2 year old down the hall when the boy wouldn't go to his mother.

Kiff told me about some three year olds who were saying those nasty words back home on Clock America. He put 'duck' tape on their mouths. He later went to all the houses that have the three year olds and ensured they had removed the 'duck' tape.

He is such a thoughtful child.

***

Just a random fact: Girls on Clock America are called Sabozos and boys are Wah-Wahs.

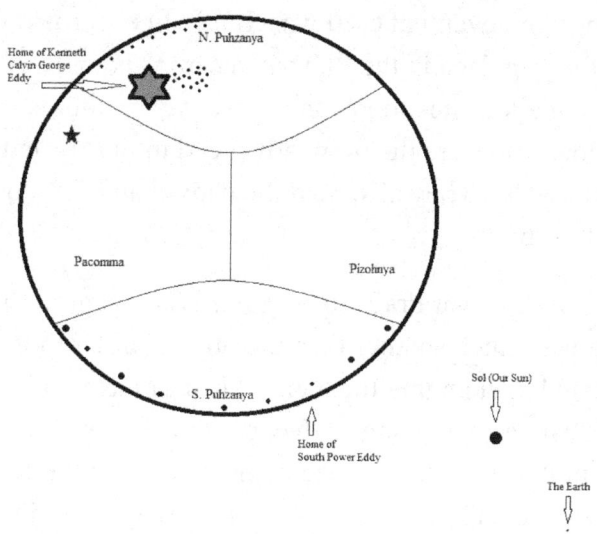

Clock America has enjoyed long periods of peace but there is a violent past. At one time the planet had no individual countries, just farming communities and independent cities. However strife erupted over what to call the land mass. Some wanted to maintain the name Pacomma (puh-comma) which had endured for many centuries. Others wished to rename the land in honor of a certain family named Puhzanya (puh-zahn-ya). He never told me why this family was so important but I think it was somehow related to the creation of pizza and ice cream.

165

The arguments grew louder to the point of violence and eventual civil war. Battle lines formed with ¾ of the populace in the Puhzanya camp and only ¼ swearing allegiance to Pacomma. However, the traditionalists were the more advanced militarily and commercially. They also held the capitol and most of the industrial might.

As the war dragged on a third faction grew. This group was much smaller than the others but far more dedicated to changing the name. Most of the populace didn't care a fig so long as they continued to eat pizza three nights a week. The newcomers believed the famous clan was actually named Pizohnya (pih-zone-ya pih sounds like "give") and broke from the larger Puhzanya coalition. Their wanton attacks on both original parties threw the entire planet into chaos.

This defection proved crucial as it shifted the balance of power so dramatically that a stalemate developed. After several decades of war a cease fire was declared. Each faction would control the lands they currently held. As can be seen by the included map, this established Pacomma on the western hemisphere, Pizohnya on the east and the Puhzanya group split into Northern and Southern districts.

Although the nations have moved beyond open warfare, some individuals continue to make raids against their old enemies. Such incursions do threaten the general peace but are looked upon as an acceptable evil so long as it doesn't interrupt the pizza delivery guy.

***

As was mentioned earlier, Pacomma is home to the traditional capitol of C.A. which is located not too far from the N. Puhzanyan border. According to Kiff, the land has "hundreds of buildings and casinos".

N. Puhzanya boasts 2060 buildings, 4 of which are knife stores (aka Home Depot *tm*). They do not seem to understand the basics of commerce as they give away all their products including wood, knives, bottles, caps and CO_2 tanks used for home carbonating.

***

The boy finally confessed the reason he considers me an anti-Clock American. As his home was located in N. Puzahnya it is fair to assume he aligned himself with that faction in the wars. I, on the other hand, was from another band. Most likely I hailed from Pacomma because I like to be in charge and rule over the technology like the TV.

167

In a fit of terrible rage, I planted a bomb in the main districts of S. Puzahnya's capitol, destroying half the city. Kenneth swore eternal hatred against me for this and has pursued me from their dying planet to this one. Forever bent on exacting revenge.

***

Kenneth's own home is also located in the North. It is a wide, spacious house almost 10 times as large as our sun. He likes throwing lavish parties and playing hockey in the kitchen. He has many neighbors, although their homes are nowhere near as nice as his own, being only about 3 times as large as the earth.

S. Puhzanya has many "homemade" stores or businesses dedicated to selling things which are homemade. It also has 9 homes. One of the homes (3rd from the east) is owned by South Power Eddy. Perhaps he's a distant relative of K.C.G.Eddy?

***

C.A. faced not only internal strife but also external enemies. On a Monday in the 1950's a massive invasion of aliens descended upon the now peaceful planet. Her inhabitants fought mightily and pushed back the oncoming hoard. Kiff was among the freedom fighters, performing heroic deeds of valor and bravery.

This was not only a matter of self-preservation but also a commitment to protect the Earth since C.A. is a much bigger planet and guardian of our home. I suppose this is a bit like the Sister City program, sharing cultural ties, commercial interests and strategic defense responsibilities.

***

Time is a very interesting topic. Whether one views it as merely a subjective construct for measuring the passage of seasons, orbits and rotations or as some metaphysical abstract which has no real meaning, we cannot deny that this planet revolves in time.

As Kiff related some history of C.A. I noticed a slight discrepancy: Either Kenneth was indeed 5-years-old as I thought or C.A.-time was wildly different from Earth-time. How could he have fought off the invasion some 60+ years ago unless the word "years" had a different meaning to him? I asked how old he was and the boy became insistent, almost indignant, that he was indeed only five. I hope to discover more about this later.

***

Kenneth and I just left a fireworks stand as we prepare to celebrate the Fourth of July, 2012. He is very excited about the potential for flames, explosions and general mayhem. Ever the inquisitive child, he just asked why we have fireworks on the Fourth.

I explained to him about the American Revolution and how our country was born in war; how we used the fireworks to remember all the cannons, rockets and bombs used during battle; and that it was a time to remember all those who fought and died for us to have our own country.

He thought for a moment and then proudly said, "I was here for the Revolution. I came from Clock America, which is a gazillion and fifty-thousand miles away, and I came just before the war started and I brought the bombs which made it possible to blow-up all the people who were fighting against us."

"Oh, so you won the war for us?" I asked.

"Yes. Yes I did."

"That's not what the history books say."

"They have it wrong."

It wouldn't be the first time.

***

As with any good story, there must be an ending. I was truly sad to hear that Clock America has been destroyed. It seems a very large bomb was placed in the center of the planet and it exploded, destroying the entire sphere. This happened in the 1980's on a Saturday. Great was my surprise and joy however to find that the Magratheans (Hitchhiker's Guide to the Galaxy) were building a new and better C.A.

No word on whether it was to be even larger but one can only hope.

***

Kiff was rather morose when telling me about the final moments of C.A. His mother (whether he meant Heather or some other Clock American woman I do not know) had become aware of the bomb and built a machine which held it in check.

One day the demons broke her machine and so the planet exploded (insert big explosive sound and 'angry hands' here). Luckily he had a portal which opened in his living room and so he was able to come to the Earth and dropped in right over this house.

***

I mentioned earlier that C.A. was part of the Star Wars universe. While those movies were "a long time ago, in a galaxy far far away", Kiff's planet is older still. We were watching *Revenge of the Sith* and Anakin was just about to attack Obi Wan for the final battle sequence. Suddenly Kiff piped-up to say, "Oh, that's Clock America."

"Really?" I asked.

"Oh yea, that's what it looked like after the bomb went off. I went to visit it and swam in the fire. That's why I can throw fire balls at my dad, whom I want to destroy."

"So I was your dad on Clock America?"

"No, he was a different dad whom I had to destroy."

"Was Mommy your mommy there?"

"Yes and she was 1000 years old."

"Well she looks pretty good for being so ancient."

"Yes and that is why I had to destroy my dad by throwing fire balls at him and using his Nerf dart gun to shoot laser darts at him at night."

I want a Nerf laser dart shooter.

***

I must confess, for a time I was sucked into the Clock America mythology. The last I heard the planet was under construction by the Magratheans but seemed to be taking quite a while. What am I saying? Only God can build a planet in six days…

Anyway, I asked how things were coming on the repairs.

"They were working but not anymore."

"Did they finish or get stuck?"

"They got stuck half way through because you (Brian) put something sticky on their wrenches."

I don't sound like a very nice person.

***

As a historian, Kenneth leaves a bit to be desired. Though informative, I do not quite trust his ability to present a full and complete biography of this amazing planet. He let slip a tiny nugget of truth which led to this conclusion…perhaps. Maybe I didn't follow the logic properly. Tell me what you think:

173

"I don't remember Clock America. I only remember the words about Clock America that are the words about what I don't remember about Clock America."

Uh…yeah. Maybe his tummy computer has a virus.

Chapter 21
Patricide

Some few days after his 5th birthday, Kiff walked into our bedroom on a cool Saturday morning and proudly announced he was going to destroy me. Naturally I was a bit bemused and so politely asked him to clarify the matter. Actually I said, "What ex-*actly* do you mean by that!?" He giggled and ran away.

I was warned. I should have paid heed to the signs. Only a fool doesn't listen when someone with the power to do so claims a mandate to kill. Foolish, foolish me.

Since that declaration of war, not a day has passed in which he has not reminded me that the days of my life were numbered. Indeed I now believe that, like Count Vladimir Harkonnen, Kenneth encompasses my doom.

I once asked him why he wants to destroy me.

His face began to glow with joy, "Because I do not remember why I came here".

SO…killing your father is the rational answer to a complete lack of purpose in one's life? Couldn't he take-up bowling or macramé?

Heather asked him how he was going to commit this heinous act. "I'm going to spank him until he can't sit down." And then giggled some more.

***

After his first feeble attempts to snuff out my life, the child sought reinforcements and enlisted his siblings into the terrible plot. One evening the older boy (who paraphrasing Mr. Cosby, 'does not wish to make it to 15'), attacked me while I lounged on the couch. He tried hard to keep my arms occupied while the 'demon spawn' ascended to the back of the sofa and leapt bodily onto my shoulders. Between the two of them I was dragged to the floor and had my head bounced against the coffee table. Alex obviously enjoyed testing himself against his father. Kenneth simply wanted to spill some blood...mine.

The child's desire to bestrip me of my mortal coil is not a constant. In fact, just the other day he proudly announced that he did not want to destroy me but help me to be stronger than the whole world. I assure you his change of heart was both temporary and motivated by self-interest as I had just given him a large bar of chocolate.

***

While there are those who think little of me, and what little they think is all bad, I do try to be a good father to my children. I feed them, clothe them and teach what minor amounts of wisdom I posses. Certainly I don't give them cause to hate me any more than the average parent of a couple teens might. None of this seems to count for much to our *sweet little schnook-ums* though.

That infamous Sunday of "those two words" fame (see chapter 18), found me lying in bed next to my wife, enjoying the languid early hours of a beautiful Sabbath morn. The refreshing scent of clean sheets mixed with roses and new mown grass blended to make me drowsy and contented. In other words, I dropped my guard.

Without warning a body flew through the air and landed squarely on my head. I simply cannot imagine how he launched himself so high or far. Perhaps I'll send the boy off to the next Summer Olympics for the high jump. What I do know is I immediately felt a deep crack in my spine and the muscles running from the base of my skull down to the left shoulder blade began to scream in agony.

I wrestled to escape this ball of hysterical laughter and was only vaguely aware Heather was not only NOT providing any help, she had somehow vacated the bed before his deadly attack. Thanks hon.

Eventually, and I'm talking after five minutes here, I managed to fling him onto the bed and run in utter panic for the bedroom door. Oh how badly did I underestimate Kiff's ability to plan his assault. Immediately outside our room the floor was strewn with 10,000 minute toys. Plastic figurines, legos, and marbles formed a very sharp and amazingly effective minefield.

During the few seconds I stood there, weighing my options, he leapt from the bed onto my back and began intertwining himself into my limbs. I tried to reach back and pull him off but a second, more devious plot had formed in that twisted little brain. This was a plan which I could neither have imagined nor wished upon another.

Tiny, thin and infinitely sharp toenails began raking into the small of my back. Little feet, undoubtedly soaked in liquid hydrogen, slipped into the waistband of my sweats. With a whoop of glee my assailant let go of my hair (by which he had been hanging) and slid neatly into the back of my pants. Quick as a flash he tossed my shirt over him and there I stood, 40 pounds of extra backside which could think for itself and thought this was the funniest thing that had ever happened.

***

Among the great difficulties in being a parent of a five year old is one can never quite feel safe. As I sat here writing I heard Kenneth in the living room, laughing. Aside from the special significance that bears for me (and the fear) it is generally not a good thing.

I caught up with the kid while he sat on the toilet.

"Kenneth, I heard you laughing earlier. Why?"

"Because I'm gonna laugh you out of this world."

I looked at him in mixed humor and trepidation. Then, to my utter horror, he began to rub his hands together exactly in the manner of classic movie villains.

"And I know just the plan."

As I listen to the flushing of a commode the level of danger rises around me. Things are turning dark. From his open bedroom door comes the click and tap of tinker toys being hastily assembled. Then the louder plastic banging of duplo blocks. Every once in a while boom the fake explosions which signify a blast against his enemies.

"I will build a machine…"

"…because he does not control me…"

"…one which will let me be invisible."

"And I shall DESTROY MY DAD!"

I ran to hide behind; I mean consult with, Heather about what we should do for the child. Surely this was neither normal nor healthy. She said it was just a thing. "He's playing." Relieved I walked down the hall and listened to him singing a song,

"…and the crunchies on your face…I'll hide the rest in the mattress."

Help.

***

Occasionally I do find some small measure of respite from this ever present danger. Just today I found Kenneth building a duplo block tower in Heather's art room. I did not even have to ask what he was doing.

"Dad"

"Yes son?"

"Do you want to know what I am building?"

"Sure"

"I am building a machine to suck out Mom's brains."

I stood there in complete shock. Partially because the very thought of sucking out a person's brains was disturbing on a great many levels but mostly because his nefarious scheme was not aimed at me.

"Why do you want to suck out Mommy's brains?" If this was not the worst question I would ever ask…

"I want to see what's on her mind."

My perpetually bemused smile returned but before I could even process this thought he continued.

"Then I will blow them back in but she's not a villain."

Which of course makes perfect sense.

***

He is telling me he will destroy me again when Heather tells him to be kind to his daddy. He leans up to my ear and whispers, "What do you want to hear?"

"I love you Daddy."

"Dad, let me tell you something…today is the destroying day."

Then he rammed his big ol' lump of a head right into my face before running away.

I hear laughing in the dark recesses of my house, back in the bedrooms. Then a voice breaks through, "Dad! Come. In. Your. Room."

"No!"

"Come in here!"

"No, you scare me."

The five year old has won.

***

Heather and I made appointments with the doctor for this afternoon. They were for after school so we had to take him with us. On the way he began to complain that he did not want to go to the doctor.

"You're not going to see the doctor Kenneth. Mommy and I need to see him."

"Why?"

"Because Mommy has an owwie on her foot and I have one on my arm."

He thought about that for a moment before asking in a giggly voice, "Did I cause the owwie on your arm?"

I think he might really hope he did.

***

His plots are varied in detail and scope. One day he is constructing a large and powerful machine designed to rip out my guts. The next I find a t-pin carefully inserted into the straw of
my drink.

Have I let this little game go too far?

***

Perhaps some metaphysical bond exists between my bathroom and the more homicidal portions of Kenneth's brain. Who knows? All I can say is more often than one might expect, I hear his plots while visiting the lavatory.

Just yesterday I was about my business when suddenly a huge booming thud echoed from outside the door.

"What the…!" I yelled.

"Daddy, you have 20 lives left."

After shoving my heart back into its usual place I realized he was continuing a previous conversation (see chapter 19).

"Oh good", I replied dryly and opened the door. "At least I have a while to live."

There in the hall stood my dear sweet youngest child, naked except for a pair of miniscule tighty-whities, mightily wielding a practice kung fu staff and prepared to strike. It was *Lord of the Flies* only lacking war paint.

The look of fear on my face must have emboldened him as he looked up at me triumphantly and declared "No, 'cause I'm gonna hit you extra special super hard and break all twenty of your lives at once."

I slowly shut the door in his face.

Oh poop.

***

It was late and I was just beginning to doze after a long day. Kenneth clambered onto the bed and wriggled next to me. I sure miss those wonderful moments when I could lie back and hold my infant son, protecting him from the evil world outside. My heart welled with joy that perhaps he had once again decided to love me.

"I love you Kenneth."

"I love you too Daddy."

This was the best day ever. What could I possibly say to show how much I adored this sweet little boy?

"Ha! You can't destroy me now!"

"Well, I'll only destroy you when you do bad things. I'll burn you in the fire for three days and then bring you back and teach you to be good."

What?! Is this some kind of "Harrowing of Hell" thing going on?

I do love these special moments with my son.

***

Kenneth loves stuffed animals and occasionally inducts them into his clandestine hit squad, the sole purpose of which is my utter demise. Today however he showed a softer side...and made me think.

"Daddy, this is Hockey Bear", he said, indicating the small white toy dressed in blue satin, a tri-color · sweater and skates. Personally I think he is more Figure Skater Bear and perhaps Interior Decorator Bear professionally, but to each his own. Kiff continued, "He's scared of you."

I have heard of children using this type of personification in order to say things they feel.

"Why is he afraid of me?"

"Because he doesn't like the spankings you give me. They hurt."

Now, I *do* understand that some in our society no longer accept the validity of corporal punishment. A few even call it child abuse. Personally I am thankful my parents walloped me as much as they did and (now) wish they had done it a bit more. I probably would not have made many of the mistakes I did later on. The difference I think is that I try to explain WHY it happens and WHY these lessons are important. My experience working in the jail also tells me many of those men never learned a simple lesson: other people have rights and you can't do whatever you want; there are consequences.

"Well", I said, choosing my words carefully, "Hockey Bear doesn't have to be afraid of me. I only give spankings when I have to. Does he know why I give them?"

"No."

"Mommies and Daddies give spankings when little children have done something wrong."

"But I don't like them."

"That is good. What we need you to learn is that some things are bad to do. If you learn that doing bad things means you will get a spanking, and you don't like spankings, then maybe you will learn to not do those bad things so you won't get a spanking."

"Well, Hockey Bear will help me stop doing those things."

I pray to God he can.

***

Kiff's resolve to be good and kind did not last long. I just walked into his room upon which he looked up maliciously and said, "Daddy, you need to go away because I am not ready for the war yet."

"And who exactly are you going to fight this war against?" As if I didn't know.

"Well, me and Mommy are going to fight against you because you have seven bad lives in you and we have to destroy them before you can be good."

"But what if I don't want to fight against you?"

"Well, you have to because you have 20 good lives but we have to get rid of your bad lives."

Viva La Revolucion!

***

Amazing how life comes full circle. One week after his birth we took Kiff to a hockey game. Now, five and a half years later we are watching game two of the 2012 Stanley Cup finals. Kiff walks up to me with a toy in his hand. It is made of these circular plastic rings with short rods on them. They can be latched onto each other like strange mutated legos. Anyway, he walks up with a large gun made of these things, points it right at my face and hisses out a "laser blast" sound.

Great, he's back to destroying me.

"Daddy, now your brain and your testicles are…"

"Kenneth! That's not nice and I don't want you talking about that."

He just stood there giving me a long appraising look.

"Now your brain and your…organs…are gone."

Well I suppose that's better than being emasculated.

***

Kenneth is sitting quietly, masticating his goldfish crackers, when I realize I have not told him recently how much I love him.

"Kenneth, ya know what?"

"What?"

"I love you."

"Daddy, ya know what?"

"What?"

"The day of our big battle is coming."

***

Later that night he approached Heather and me.

"Kenneth", she asked, "Don't you love Daddy?"

"Yes. But we are going to have a battle…and it's going to be on a Saturday."

Because of course, good Christians don't commence their wars on Sunday.

***

It seems this looming battle is never far from his mind. The next day, as I was writing this very chapter, he ran into the office and gave me a wonderful (though momentary) surprise.

"Daddy, I love you!"

"Oh, Kenneth, thank you. I love you too. But this is sure a change. Why do you love me now?"

"Mommy told me to say that. But we are still going to have a battle someday. But you are too strong to go to my school so I will have to take all your power. I will take all but one drop of your power and then we can have our battle and I will defeat you."

***

Like any good soldier, Kenneth is often in training for the eventual battle. He even makes the occasional sortie just to see how I might react, testing the defenses as it were. Certain dads must keep on their toes lest they fall victim to assassination attempts.

I was in the kitchen preparing a pizza when I heard the quiet patter of feet behind me. I listened closely and picked-up a soft mutter.

"I will get close to him and poke his bottom."

Instantly I felt a finger hit my right cheek, followed by raucous laughter. I turned to see a very naked 5-year-old running away, flush with the joy of a successful reconnaissance mission.

I chased him out the door and returned to my cooking. A few seconds later the sound of bare feet slapping the kitchen tile once again graced my ears. It seem funny he would try again and I prepared to spin around and "boo" him.

He drew closer. I thought, "Just a few feet more and…"

I spun on my heel to find a 6 foot long wooden rod pointed not three inches from my nose. I jumped back in surprise and he, once again the victor, ran away laughing hysterically.

***

For the last several weeks Kenneth has been obsessed with the Tron movies. He talks constantly about whether someone is a program or a user and especially about de-rezzing me. For those who have not seen the movies, that means killing.

Just now he walked up to me, looked me right in the face and said, "Dad, you're really smart. But not smart enough to de-rez *me*."

We'll see. I think I'll put him on the Game Grid.

***

In war each side scores victories. Kenneth earned one last night. I lay in my room half asleep when suddenly came a rattling at the foot of the bed. I ignored it, too tired to care. Then I felt a cool plastic ring settle on the toes of my right foot. Kiff was playing with his hula-hoop again.

Still awake enough to play for a second, I grasped the ring with my big toe and waited for his frustrated tugging to get it back. Instead, he grabbed my left foot, hooked the ring into that big toe so I was now wearing one giant 'toe cuff' and began to yell.

"Success!!!! My plan has worked! Now my dad is kip-tured and I shall go on to victory!"

191

Drat, drat and double-drat.

Chapter 22
The Apple Doesn't Fall Far From the Tree

My mother passed away earlier this year after a long and painful illness. Her grandchildren were one of the few joys that remained to her as the end neared. She loved all of them with a profound and abiding devotion. I am so very thankful she got to know Kenneth for at least a few years.

As the boy's personality developed, Mom kept telling me, "He's just like you were." I never believed her. How could he be? I am an intellectual. I think deeply about a whole range of topics and take seriously the challenges of life. This boy is a wild spirit who flits from one idea to another without the slightest gossamer thread connecting them. Surely I was never so tenuously tied to reality. At least that is what I thought until last weekend.

Dad brought me a large plastic crate full of things Mom had collected over the years. Not until Sunday afternoon did I begin sorting through the papers I found inside. Mostly it was old school work and Cub Scout awards. But as I dug deeper a few of the pieces began to catch my eye.

***

I can remember drawing this. Why is lost to history but it certainly reminds me of something Kiff

would do. And that is a <u>lot</u> of "dynomit".

***

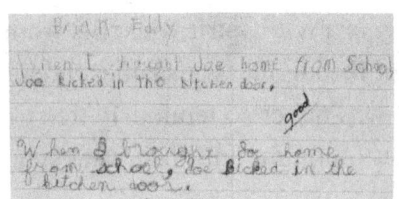

When I brought Joe home from school, Joe kicked in the kitchen door.

Reading this piece, not knowing who the author was, my first question would be, "Is this child being abused?" And why didn't the teacher ask about my choice of friends to bring home? Just so you know, I never saw anyone kick in the kitchen door. You couldn't, they were pocket doors.

***

This reminds me of a note found near the bottom of the crate. I wrote to my mom asking if I could go with her on an errand. My reasons were very clear and (I think) persuasive: 1) We would have a lot of fun. 2) Gena (my sister) would be bored without me. 3) If she made me stay home then my brothers Damon and Willie would hurt me because they always did whenever she left.

***

Remember back in chapter 20 when we visited Clock America? I thought Kenneth had finally cracked. What kid makes-up something like that? Surely that came from his mother right? I thought so too, until I found a nifty little painting I did in Kindergarten which is duly titled: The Ice Cream Planet Exploding.

To paraphrase Aunt Marge, "Genetics will out".

***

Much like Kenneth, I loved my mother. She wasn't perfect and I was aware of that from an early age. To the best of my recollection I never said I wanted to marry her. Though a boy could do worse than to become espoused to as good, wise and dedicated a woman as my mom. So it is not surprising I sent her a Valentine's Day card every year.

I think the tone and visuals in this one finally answer the question asked at the beginning of this book. Yes, Kenneth is all my fault.

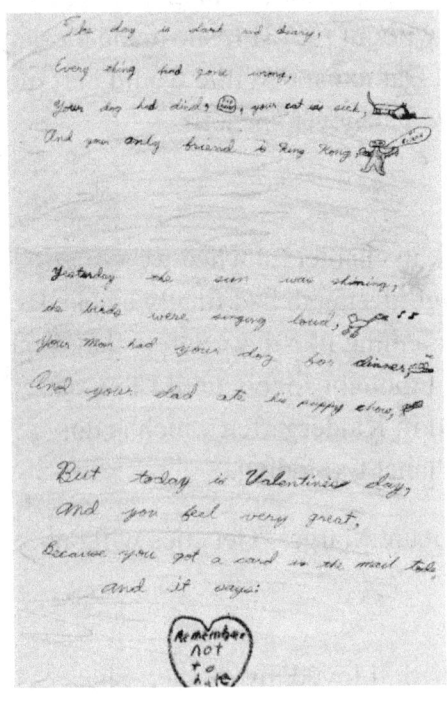

The day is dark and dreary,
Every thing had gone wrong,
Your dog had died (rip rover), your cat is sick,
And your only friend is King Kong (hi friend).

Yesturday the sun was shining,
The birds were singing loud,
Your mom had your dog for dinner (woof),
And your dad ate his puppy chow.

But today is Valentine's Day
And you feel very great,
Because you got a card in the mail today,
And it says, "Remember not to hate".

Chapter 23
Fangs for the Memories

Some tales of 'The Kiffster' don't fit neatly into any of these chapters so here are a few completely random tidbits.

***

(Heather)

Thursday, October 22, 2009 Literary Boy

The other day I was talking to Kiff, trying to use my time as a Mommy wisely by having a teaching moment.

"What sound does a doggie make?" I asked.

"Ruff ruff!" Kiff answered.

"What sound does a kitty make?"

He hesitated, although I know he knows what sound a kitty makes. "Meow," I prompted. "Meow! Meow!" Kiff chimed.

Thinking that I had to help now, I said, "What sound does a cow make?" and said, "Moo-ooo!" with him.

"What sound does a pig make? Oink oink!"

"NO Mommy! Pigs say, Not by the hair of my chinny-chin-chin!"

***

In the utter chaos that is the Eddy home at bedtime, Heather picked Kenneth up, gave him a huge hug and asked, "Kenneth, do you love me?"

"Yes", he said in a bright and heartfelt voice. Then added in the slight growl used by all maniacal dictators-in-training, "But you are my slave."

Then he began to lurch back and forth in her arms crying aloud, "All hail me! All hail me!"

I sat and watched the unfolding spectacle in the same shocked awe that Mr. and Mrs. Stalin surely must have felt at Young Josef's first attempt to collectivize his kindergarten class.

***

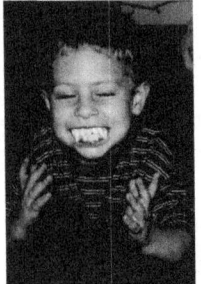

Halloween is such a fixture in the American culture I feel I can say with some confidence that everyone has tried out a pair of plastic vampire fangs and uttered those immortal

198

words, "I vahn to sahk yo blahd". I've done it and you have too. Don't deny the truth. You know you have.

Kenneth found a pair one day and we couldn't extract them for almost a week. I threatened to take him to the dentist but he doesn't know to be afraid of them yet so my bluff passed by idly.

For several days I had to check behind every door and under each blanket lest that fierce Undead Being were to attack me while unawares. Of course we had a rather effective defense against 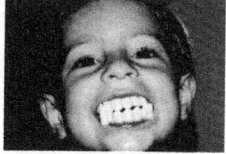 him. If we fixed the dread creature in the eye and held its gaze for but a few seconds, he would collapse into a fit of laughter, allowing our escape. Better still, tickling would cause his teeth to fall from his mouth completely, thus rendering him completely harmless.

***

We're fans of the Harry Potter franchise. The books are voraciously consumed by every member of the family. We cannot go a week without seeing one of the movies. I've even begun writing two pieces of fan fiction (one is about a father reading the books to his young witch in the summer before she goes to Hogwarts and the second is about the origins of the Goblet of Fire). We also LOVE butter beer.

Go online and you will find dozens of recipes for the foamy, warming treat which features so prominently in the stories. Once I bought a carbon dioxide tank and could make my own soda, I began to experiment with the available potions. Those with whom I have shared a bottle or two seem to think it rather tasty. Except of course for Kenneth.

Today is the Fourth of July and I made four 2-liter bottles for our celebration. When Kiff walked into the kitchen I pointed out my creation and asked if he knew what it was.

"No, what?" he answered.

"Butter beer."

"Bleech", he croaked.

"But you like my butter beer."

"I like the butter beer you don't make. I don't like the butter beer you do make."

I'm rather bummed.

***

So Heather tells Kenneth to get ready for bed and brush his teeth. Surprisingly, he did. When came back with the announcement that as he "had clean teeth [he] didn't need to swish [his] mouth with soda."

She asked him, "Guess what's next."

"What?"

She sang, "You won't like it."

"It doesn't matter", he sang back.

"Go to bed!"

He whispered, "It matters".

***

Kenneth, like me, was born a blond and grew darker with time. Just a few moments ago he and Heather had an interesting conversation.

"Kenneth, your hair is getting darker."

"No it isn't."

He then began tugging on his hair and craning his neck trying to get a look at his dirty blond locks. Failing to see them properly he ran into the hallway where he could examine himself properly in the mirror. The instant he saw the brown strands poking out of his head he exclaimed, "Oh My!!"

***

Occasionally what comes out of his mouth is so random one simply has no response. Heather and Kenneth are cooking their dinner and I roamed in just to spend a few seconds with them. She looked at me in a state of utter bewilderment and said, "Kenneth says he wants two heads so he can eat chicken nuggets and French fries at the same time."

"From McDonald's", he was careful to add.

That goes without saying.

***

We like to sprinkle our conversations with movie quotes. A sort of game has developed with the speaker getting points for most appropriate usage and whether anyone else can guess the character and movie.

For example, when I am feeling particularly worn out and someone comments on my getting old, I will respond with: "Honey, it's not the age…it's the mileage."

For those who don't recognize it, picture Indiana Jones and Marion on the tramp steamer during Raiders of the Lost Ark. He is groaning in pain after fighting the huge bald guy on the plane and then commandeering the truck. She tells him to stop acting like a baby (as I remember).

Kenneth is an enthusiastic participant in this game. Granted, he rarely guesses the quote, but he will shout out with the best. Late one evening Heather is lying in bed reading when through the house rings our child's voice:

"Mommy, where do you buy a tank?"

"Uh…Wal-Mart."

"Yeeeeesssssssssss!"

Believe me, this is very funny if you have ever heard *The Mountie Song* by The Arrogant Worms.

***

Of all the members of my family, it seems Kenneth has the best rhythm. Or I should rather say, 'He is the most willing to move to his own rhythm'. We were listening to some music when *Funkytown* by Lipps Inc. came on.

Kiff got very excited and called to Heather, "Mommy, it's your work song!"

"My work song?"

"Yes! I just made it your work song."

'*Disco while you work…Da-doo-doo doo doo doo*'

***

The boy watches far too much TV while at the sitter's. Heather and I decided not to have cable. The few programs we wanted to watch were overwhelmed by all the filth and tripe. It just wasn't worth the harm of bringing it into our home not to mention *paying for it*. Kenneth however soaks up every bit he can.

We heard a tsunami washing over the tub during his bath last night. I poked my head in to see him squeezing the bar of soap out of his hands and then launching himself bodily after it.

He noticed me and asked, "Daddy, why is this so slippery? I can't hold it tight."

"Well Kiff, it is soap and soap is made that way."

He looked at me with pitying eyes and carefully explained that, "It's not soap. It's Dove, 1/4 moisturizing cream."

Thanks Unilever.

***

From Heather's Facebook page:

Kiff just informed me that he needs to find a girl his age who loves him so he can date her. He will take her to dinner at "a place."

***

She reminded me of the times when Kenneth wanted to share my bath. For many months he would rush into the bathroom whenever he heard the water running. I was working my way through online school and the last thing I needed was a naked toddler clambering into the tub while I was trying to compose an essay.

Heather said whistfully, "You were number one in his life then."

Obviously the kid was listening from his room because just then a soft and faintly amused voice drifted across the hall, "You're number zero now."

***

Later in the conversation I began to laugh at my faint memories of the show *Sanford and Son*. My wife asked what was so funny. I explained about Redd Foxx and how he was filthy but sooo hilarious. Of course I tossed out the line, "Don't be a..." when Kenneth shouted, "Hey dad! Don't be a dummy dummy!"

My boy.

***

He has begun telling us about his dreams. Mostly they are about candy or playing at the park. But every once in a while the night visions are slightly more traumatic:

"Daddy, let me tell you about my dream."

> *Satan put a giant shark*
> *into our house and it ate*
> *just a tiny little bit of me.*
> *Then it went and ate a*
> *whole great big bit of you.*
> *So I went a built a machine*
> *in my room that was way*
> *powerful so it could kill*
> *that shark. But it didn't kill*
> *the shark and so I took a*
> *great big knife and*
> *chopped it in half.*

I'm not sure what the symbolism is. At least he was protecting me this time.

***

Kenneth and I headed home after returning Alex and Mack to their mom. We were both rather sad, knowing we would not see them again for a week. Little sobs of anguish echoed through our small car. I wanted to reach back and comfort him. After a big sniff he cleared his throat and announced, "Hey, I can see New Jersey from here!"

We live in Southern California.

***

Later that evening I tried once again to earn Kiff's love. Just before bed I gave him a huge hug and said, "I love you buddy."

He twisted, squirmed and shoved my face away. Then in a most serious tone replied, "Stay away from me. You have Beard and Mustache disease."

***

My dad offered to take Alex and me to a minor league baseball game. Someone wondered if Kenneth was going to go. From out of the kitchen floated Heather's voice, "No, because no one likes him."

Alex laughed. Kenneth screamed. I choked out, "That's so harsh."

She walked into the living room and said, "Oh he knows it's not true. Don't you Kenneth?"

"No it's not true!" he yelled. "But it was truly evil."

***

Heather shared one with me this morning:

Kenneth was sooo funny earlier. He came bouncing into the room and then stopped with a look of utter horror on his face.

"I didn't wake you up did I?" he asked.

"No Kiff, I was already awake."

"Good", he said obviously relieved. Then he saw one of our cats on the bed and added, "Oh, hello kitty. I

207

want to pet you and scratch you and love you. But *mommy* threw that pillow on you so don't bite *me*."

***

Kenneth started school a couple weeks ago. Unlike many children, he had no separation anxiety at all. Off he ran into the school yard with nary a look back. When we got him home that afternoon the first words out of his mouth were, "Mommy, guess what? I didn't get sent to the office even once!"

Frankly, I'm a little surprised.

***

He spent the first day cutting into the front of the line whenever his class moved through the halls. He simply *had* to walk next to the teacher holding her hand.

***

Homework began a couple days in and he quickly decided it wasn't for him.

"Daddy, why do I have to do homework?"

"So you can learn and be smart so you can get a good job when you grow up and afford a very nice retirement home for Mommy and me."

"I'll earn a gazillion dollars and buy Mommy a palace. You can be her servant and bring her ice cream and cookies for breakfast."

***

On Thursday evening Heather told Kenneth to get ready for bed early.

"Why do I have to get ready for bed? I want to stay up and do my puzzles."

"Because I have to take you to Aunt Francie's early tomorrow. I have to go to work early and you have to go to school."

"What if your boss said (in a deep manly voice), 'There's no work today. Go home.' And then my teacher said, 'There's no school today. Go home.' And then we could stay home and have fun."

"I'm afraid that will never happen Kenneth. There's always something to do."

He thought for just a second and then responded, "But it *could* happen."

***

Kenneth is a tickler. Yesterday he slipped behind the counter at the local "stop-n-rob" gas station and began to tickle the female clerk. Heather told him to stop and keep his hands to himself. He complained that that would make the store like school with all the rules and he didn't like that.

***

The fun and games didn't stop at the Fastrip either. We went to church this morning and Kenneth attacked three separate older ladies. They all laughed and thought he was cute. I think he's playing the field.

***

If you ever meet him say, "Hey Kiff, tell me a story." Who knows what you'll hear.

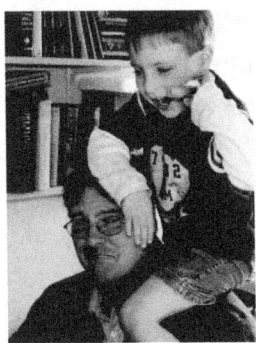

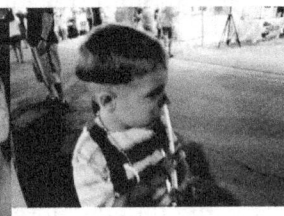

Acknowledgements

This book would have been nothing but blank pages without the extraordinary imagination and creativity of my dear son Kenneth. I Love You.

Thank you, Heather. You allowed me to disappear into this project for hours on end. A lesser woman would have worn us both out with complaints.

While editing for publication, I asked Heather if it was okay to use the word "boobies". She said no, the book didn't need it and besides, "grown-ups don't say 'boobies'." I said, "We don't run in the same circles of grown-ups." Boobies Boobies Boobies.

To my children Alex and Mack: I'm sorry for thinking you were both "nutty as squirrel poo". I see now it *is* genetic. There was nothing you could have done.

Last, to my mother Joan. She taught me long ago to embrace whatever talents one has. Even the most trivial skill can be valuable if used in the right way.

The End

Made in the USA
Monee, IL
10 November 2025

34200677R00118